The Jossey-Bass Nonprofit Sector Series also includes:

Rosso on Fund Raising

Rosso on Fund Raising

Lessons from a Master's
Lifetime Experience

Henry A. Rosso

Jossey-Bass Publishers • San Francisco

Substantial discounts on bulk quantities of Jossey-Bass books are available to corporations, professional associations, and other organizations. For details and discount information, contact the special sales department at Jossey-Bass Inc., Publishers (415) 433–1740; Fax (800) 605–2665.

For sales outside the United States, please contact your local Simon & Schuster International Office.

 Manufactured in the United States of America on Lyons Falls Pathfinder Tradebook. This paper is acid-free and 100 percent totally chlorine-free.

Library of Congress Cataloging-in-Publication Data

Rosso, Henry A., date.
   Rosso on fund raising : lessons from a master's lifetime experience / Henry A. Rosso.
      p.   cm. — (The Jossey-Bass nonprofit sector series)
   Includes bibliographical references and index.
   ISBN 0-7879-0304-3 (acid-free paper)
   1. Fund raising. I. Title. II. Series.
HG177.R674 1996
361.7′068′1—dc20
                                                     96-25320

FIRST EDITION
HB Printing 10 9 8 7 6 5 4 3 2 1

The Jossey-Bass Nonprofit Sector Series

Contents

Preface

This book has been in my mind for many years. It is an effort to transfer to others thoughts I have accumulated and stored over nearly half a century in the service of fund raising. It also is intended to communicate the technical fundamentals and the theoretical basics that I have been teaching in the classroom for more than twenty years. However, although I do direct my attention to some basic principles and techniques, I am more concerned with the heritage of fund raising: the wisdom bequeathed by the giants of the past, the idea of stewardship, and the place of integrity in the structure and work of philanthropy and in the profession of fund raising. In this book, I have tried to address the traditions that provided the building blocks for the structure in which we work today and also to pass along telling professional memories and the important lessons I have learned.

Audience

The audience for this book includes students of fund raising; development officers and staff; and executives, trustees, and volunteers—that is, all those interested in studying philanthropic fund raising at its working, conceptual, and philosophical levels. For each reader, there will be lessons on every page, both directly stated and contained in examples and experiences.

Overview of the Contents

Rosso on Fund Raising is divided into two parts. The eight chapters in Part One address the fundamental elements of fund raising. Chapter One, "Setting Realistic Expectations," is a case history, with many lessons for the beginning practitioner and reminders for the experienced professional.

Chapter Two, "Growing a Successful Fund Raising Program," examines the evolution of the fund raising program as it progresses from beginning efforts to maturity—or in the worst case, to the dismal failure and the deadly state of R.I.P. New and veteran development officers will benefit from the analysis of opportunities, stumbling blocks, and threats as well as of glorious advancement in the unfolding adventure of fund raising. This chapter's rationale is that it is wise for fund raisers to study the process before experiencing it.

Chapter Three, "Developing Leadership for Fund Raising," has grown out of my sense that there will be a growing need in the decades ahead for development officers, agency executives, and trustees to understand more fully the functional dynamics of the critical process of enlisting, orienting, involving, and expanding the cadre of leaders who are in service to fund raising and the volunteers to support them.

Chapter Four, "The Art of Asking with Composure," examines the solicitation process by testing why people give, why they do not give, and why people do not like to ask for money. It then offers time-tested tips for asking for money with composure, with confidence that you will succeed.

Chapter Five, "It's All About Being Friends: Cultivating Donors," is especially important because it describes acquiring, renewing, upgrading, and retaining precious donors. Nine-year-old Sam Henderson offers cogent advice on this matter.

In Chapter Six, "Diversifying Funding Sources," a veteran fund raiser joins us to examine the important differences that separate these two financial transactions: asking for a gift from an individual and asking for a grant from a foundation or a corporation. As in all human endeavors, there are both benefits and drawbacks, obstacles and opportunities for fund raisers working with each of these sources. Each has its unique culture and its own decision process. It is wise to learn as much as possible about that culture and decision process before making any solicitation.

Chapter Seven, "Classic Mistakes and Their Lessons," urges practitioners to walk to "the end of the branch," walk until you hear the wood beginning to crack. Dare to make mistakes because they will teach you to do things differently, to experiment, to test new and unfamiliar theses. Examples are given of lessons learned through mistakes.

Chapter Eight, "Evaluating Fund Raising Programs and Capabilities," pursues a theme drawn from Peter Drucker's extensive writings about management, evaluation, and change. His thesis that we should at times "abandon all knowledge" means, simply, that we should open our minds to new thoughts and new concepts, we should be willing to accept change. "Challenge the process" is an imperative enjoining you to keep your work pertinent to the moment. Evaluate and renew your ideas. Abandon all knowledge, and be prepared to accept new thoughts engendered by change. Read this chapter and then take stock of your program.

Part Two of this book discusses the history and theory underlying the fund raising profession. Chapter Nine, "Our Heritage: Rich in Values and Virtues," looks back to medieval England and to our own colonial era, to the writings of Cotton Mather and Benjamin Franklin, to present the wisdom bequeathed by many others in our past to guide us in our work today.

Chapter Ten, "A Blend of Art and Science: The Five Essential Steps in Disciplined Fund Raising," ventures to enter the popular debate whether fund raising is an art or a science. The reader, I hope, will be induced to join in this debate.

Chapter Eleven, "Language and the Gentle Art of Persuasion," reaches back to medieval Europe to track the genesis of the language of fund raising. The color that our choice of language gives to our solicitations is intriguing to some fund raisers, bothersome to others. Knowing the genesis and the evolution of fund raising language can help fund raisers be more precise when discussing their programs and purposes with our stakeholders.

Chapter Twelve, "My Start in Fund Raising," addresses this history from a personal angle. I am often asked how I began in this profession, and this chapter records my introduction to broad-scale, serious fund raising and to directing a major campaign, the Mothers' March on polio in 1951 in Syracuse, New York.

Chapter Thirteen, "Stewardship in Giving and Receiving," examines the thesis of stewardship, its meaning and its application to philanthropy and fund raising and to the development staff, executive team, trustees, and contributors.

Chapter Fourteen, "Recollections by One Who Was There," reaches back 168 years. For both veterans and younger fund raisers, there will be a touch of nostalgia in the story reprinted in this chapter, written in 1828 when college fund raisers and others were called "beggars."

Chapter Fifteen, "A Call to Service," was added to provoke discussion. I hope that it succeeds. For all of us, is fund raising a call to serve the public good, or is it just a job?

Acknowledgments

It would be unusual for an author to complete a book drawing upon years of experience without harboring a sincere feeling of obligation to a number of people, individuals who willingly lent their talent in offering content suggestions. I am grateful to consultant Arthur Frantzreb in McLean, Virginia, for his bestowed wisdom; retired Lilly Endowment executive Charles Johnson; Bill Somerville, president of the Philanthropic Ventures Foundation, Berkeley, California; Dean Schooler, president of the Schooler Family Foundation in Boulder, Colorado; consultant Karla A. Williams in St. Paul, Minnesota; Martha Taylor, vice president of the University of Wisconsin Foundation; consultant Gary Wolff, Mill Valley, California, who patiently read my copy to polish the language and correct the typos; Susan Munro, who coaxed the computer to accept the text; and Michael Schuetz, who tamed the computer.

I also offer my thanks to many other fund raising colleagues who encouraged me to try my hand at expressing my private thoughts about this remarkable phenomenon called fund raising.

Most of all, I must express my deepest gratitude to the one person who tolerated me when the computer and its unwilling companion, the printer, decided that they had had enough of each other and of my words and just simply quit working. Dottie, my patient, competent wife, quietly took over, solved the problem, and prodded me on to finish the manuscript—so that she could complete the task of proofreading. Without her, there would have been no book.

San Rafael, California   Henry A. Rosso
July 1996

The Author

Henry A. Rosso was the founding director of The Fund Raising School, now a program of the Center on Philanthropy at Indiana University, Indianapolis. He has been a fund raising practitioner for forty-seven years, having started his career in 1949 as vice president of Doug Johnson Associates, a public relations company in Syracuse, New York. He received his B.A. degree magna cum laude (1949) in English and journalism from Syracuse University, where he was made a member of Phi Beta Kappa and of the Delta Sigma Chi journalism honor fraternity.

From 1959 to 1972, Rosso was West Coast vice president and a member of the board of directors of the G. A. Brakeley Company, a national fund raising company. He resigned to set up his own consulting office in San Francisco and to start The Fund Raising School. In 1985, the National Society of Fund Raising Executives (NSFRE) presented Rosso with its Outstanding Fund Raising Executive Award. He has received honorary doctorates from both Pacific Union College and Indiana University. In 1990, Indiana University recognized his contributions to the advancement of philanthropy by creating the Henry A. Rosso Medal, awarded annually to a fund raising professional for lifetime achievement in ethical fund raising. Rosso was the first recipient of this award. He is also lead author of the textbook *Achieving Excellence in Fund Raising: A Comprehensive Guide to Principles, Strategies, and Methods,* published in 1991 by Jossey-Bass and winner of the NSFRE's 1992 Staley/Robeson/Ryan/St. Lawrence Prize for Research on Fund Raising and Philanthropy.

Rosso on Fund Raising

Part One

The Essentials of Fund Raising

| **Setting Realistic Expectations**

Let me begin with a true story. Three forces met one day not too long ago to deliberate on an issue of strategic importance to the future stability of a relatively small human services center in a northern U.S. city with a population of 235,000.

The primary force was the center's chief executive. The secondary force was chair of the finance committee of the board of trustees. The third force, also important, was an eager applicant to fill the recently vacated position of director of development. This candidate was particularly interested in working with an agency serving young people.

The chief executive, a competent, responsible administrator, was troubled that the center had been unable to increase its annual income to meet all the needs of its continuing, imaginative programs. Additionally, certain trustees were making noises to the effect that they were not impressed with fund raising program progress in keeping abreast of the cash flow demands generated by an ambitious board-imposed growth pattern. "If you can't do it yourself," the finance committee chair had directed the executive, "hire a competent fund raiser and put that person to work immediately gathering gift funds."

Attempting to follow that directive, the center had hired three development officers over a period of four years. Each had lacked extensive experience in broad-based major gifts fund raising and in prospect research and in constituency development. Minimum funds were raised through the usual special events: galas, mailings to the community, and routine solicitation of the governing board members by letter and of the center's staff by casual request. The final results of such annual fund raising did not merit any major communitywide celebration.

The executive felt a twinge of guilt, recalling the debacles of previous fund raising campaigns. The memory was a bitter one to the executive, who had no fund raising experience. She now realized that she had no measuring stick to determine whether or not a fund raising plan had any merit, was applicable to the needs of the organization, and was appropriate to its constituency. Nor did she know whether candidates for the development position had the knowledge or experience to put a plan in place to raise the funds required. Perhaps it was time, she had determined, to hire a self-starter, a go-getter, a person competent to increase foundation and corporate support and to promote major gifts. The chief executive knew that board members would not participate in any fund raising, particularly in the giving or getting part of it. If it is to be done, she had thought to herself, it will have to be done by the new fund raising hire. I hope that she or he has the gumption to take this on. I certainly do not have the time or the inclination to get involved myself. And she had told herself, as a sorrowful afterthought, There is no way that I can induce the board to get involved, unfortunately. Certainly, I do not want to repeat last year's painful encounter with the board.

Coming Face to Face with Reality

The fund raising candidate at the meeting was anxious to find a permanent position, one that would give her an opportunity to utilize her creative talents to the utmost, one that would exploit her ability to identify with people and to work in empathy with volunteers. She lacked hands-on experience, but she believed that she could learn the "tricks" of fund raising quite easily. After all, how complicated could it be, particularly for a person who had just completed advanced management studies?

The executive was by now convinced that the strategy had to be to pick the right person, primarily someone who needs the job. Put the person to work; don't interfere in any way. Let the person do what she or he is capable of doing.

The scene for disaster was set.

When the meeting got under way, the executive supposed that before her sat the savior capable of relieving her of the horrid responsibility of fund raising. Both the executive and the candidate anticipated that this was a decisive moment. A new era of fund raising productivity for the human services center was at hand. Because the executive was anxious to hire, she did not ask many questions of the candidate. If she had, she would have learned that this person, though eager and well intended, had minimum hands-on fund raising experience in the critical area of major gifts solicitation. However, the executive was impressed that the candidate had completed advanced studies in nonprofit management and had attended several two-hour seminars on fund raising principles offered by a community college nearby. These courses, however, were conducted by the academic faculty, and the few practical exercises assigned were not adequate to build the confidence bank necessary for individuals who must effectively solicit major gifts.

Because the candidate was eager to settle into a wage earner's mode, she, too, had few questions. Primarily, she asked, "What will be the salary?" "What benefits do you offer?" "What is the vacation period?" "Can I expect to be considered for raises in the future if I do well?" And then, almost as an afterthought, "What will you expect of me?"

The executive responded to the latter question: "Our goal will have to be $55,000 in annual fund support for the fiscal year ahead and then a steady increase in annual funds in each of the years after that. Do you feel competent to accomplish that?"

There was a tense moment of silence, and then the candidate announced, "I would like to apply for the job. I organized a campus program and raised funds working with volunteers to continue the program. I helped to raise funds for my church for three consecutive years. We made the goal. I studied fund raising principles as part of my advanced studies. I believe that I can do what you want me to do. And I can be available to start at your convenience. Can we talk for a few moments more about salary and benefits and opportunities for future advancements?"

Questions to Be Asked

This meeting was a travesty—innocent, yes, but still a travesty too often repeated: a not-for-profit organization is eager to hire an experienced person to plan and to manage the fund raising program, thereby releasing the executive from what can be a heavy responsibility for a busy person. It often would be too heavy a burden for the chief executive to carry the weight of day-to-day management as well as the custody of fund raising, to plan and to direct what many consider a nuisance, an unpleasant job that has to be done. Thus, eagerness sometimes supersedes wisdom. Eager to hire, the executive does not study the candidate's experience, does not ask for evidence of that experience, does not ask probing questions about the candidate's thoughts regarding annual fund programs or about the candidate's record in planning and directing such programs.

A sincere, often young hopeful, eager for employment and willing to do what is required but lacking the basic experience to make things happen in a complex setting, does not ask the probing questions that will help her or him determine whether or not the goal is realistic and can be attained. Does the candidate have a right to ask such questions? The candidate not only has the right to ask, she or he has a responsibility, to herself or himself and to the organization, to request responses. What questions are appropriate? If the candidate applying to the human services center described here had asked the questions that follow and heard the answers shown, these answers should have prodded her concern.

Q: What was the annual fund goal last year?
A: $40,000.
Q: How much was actually raised?
A: $32,000.
Q: How can you justify a current year goal of $55,000 when only $32,000 was raised against a goal of $40,000 last year? That is $23,000, or more than a 50 percent increase over last year's accomplishment.
A: The hard fact is that we need that kind of money to fund the programs for the fiscal year ahead.
Q: What kind of support will I be able to expect from the board members in the matter of prospect identification and solicitation?
A: Judging from past experience, relatively little performance can be expected from the board members in the annual fund

effort. They believe that this is the responsibility of the staff fund raiser.

Q: Before I say whether I think I can attain your goal of $55,000, will you permit me to study the final report of last year's annual fund program and the number of gifts produced in what amounts from what sources and equally to study the incidence of volunteer involvement in the annual fund program?

A: [*Possible answer 1.*] By all means. The information is available to you providing that you respect the confidentiality of the file information.

[*Possible answer 2, the probable answer.*] By no means. They are confidential records open only to executive staff and the board of trustees.

Q: [*Response to answer 2.*] If the files cannot be made available to me, can you give me a statistical record of total gifts received by sources, by amounts from the top-level gifts to the smallest ones? Will you permit me a day or so to study that report so that I can make an independent determination as to whether or not your goal can be reached?

These are important questions. Availability of this data would have enabled this candidate to determine the strategies that she would employ to attract the major gifts important to the success of the program. As a matter of fact, if a candidate does not ask questions about the previous annual fund, she or he simply cannot know whether sufficient valid prospects are available for major gifts solicitation.

However, this candidate applied for the job not knowing what questions to ask during the interview and what areas to examine to look for danger signs. She needed to inform herself about the extent of support that would be provided by the chief executive, the executive staff, and the board members and other volunteers. But she hesitated to test whether or not a goal of $55,000 for the annual fund program was realistic. She hesitated to ask questions about the performance of the annual fund in the previous year: What was the goal and how much was actually raised? She hesitated to probe for fear that the executive might consider her concern a weakness. And yet, how else can a candidate for development officer determine whether or not the task required can be done?

What evidence can be made available to demonstrate that the annual fund, capital, special gifts, or endowment goals that a candidate is eager to accomplish can be reached? Does a new development officer take the chief executive's assignment on in good faith, to prove that the goal can be accomplished? Or should she or he pause, while still a job applicant, to request the privilege of examining the statistics awaiting in the donor base, in order to decide whether the goal is reasonable? Reckless bravado at this moment can be costly. It may be the beginning of a long and pleasant or long and painful moment of truth. To ask the hard questions at the moment the relationship is being forged is not presumptuous. It is a responsible, honest necessity. A candidate's request for critical information before the relationship is established gives evidence that she or he is a trustworthy person, a person of integrity, who wants to do what will serve the organization well and will enable her or him to perform as a responsible professional.

The End of the Story

The long and short of my tale is that the candidate was offered the job as the center's development director, with the primary charge to raise $55,000 in annual funds during the fiscal year. She failed to meet the annual fund goal, raising only $37,000. Accordingly, she was terminated. After the fact, she discovered that the organization had raised only $32,000 in annual funds during the previous year. The expanded goal of $55,000 for the current fiscal year had not been, could not have been, justified. Facts gathered from the donor base and past fund raising history showed that a $23,000 increase in gift fund production was unlikely to be achieved by a new, untested professional. The annual fund goal had been set based solely on the premise that a new professional fund raiser would be able to create the magic that would deliver an almost 50 percent increase in annual fund production. Obviously, this did not happen. It rarely does.

Moreover, it is inevitable that failure of this nature should produce an atmosphere of acrimony, a finger-pointing athletic event, with each side valiantly trying to avoid the uncomfortable truth in the matter. Failure is difficult to accept.

Basic Requirements of Fund Raising

There is a maxim that has endured the ages and gives proper definition to the function of fund raising: "Fund raising is a simple process but a demanding taskmaster." A companion truth has been expressed by direct marketing genius Roger Craver: "You can raise considerably more money with organized fund raising than you can with disorganized fund raising" (personal communication, June 1992).

Organized fund raising is a discipline that requires cooperation from each component of the organization that is endeavoring to support its programs through volunteer gift giving. It cannot be the total effort of one person. The task is too complex. The organization seeking the funds must put its support behind the person charged with the responsibility to prepare the plan and to administer the action required by the plan.

In this case, the finance committee position was naïve ("If you can't do it by yourself, hire a competent fund raiser and put that person to work immediately gathering funds"). Fund raising is not "harvesting" the yields of nature. A fund raising professional does not simply "gather funds" scattered randomly about the landscape. Fund raising requires research, planning, recruitment and training of volunteers, identification of potential givers, and assignment of prospects to trained volunteer solicitors. Systems must be established to permit proper gift recording and acknowledgment and gift renewal and upgrading.

The casual approach to the task of raising annual funds, as stated by the finance committee chair and echoed by the executive, failed. A number of development officers presumably tried their hand at fashioning order out of possible disorder, failed, and were terminated. The first year's failure should have sounded the alarm that problems existed and would have to be identified, diagnosed, and disposed of before any developmental effort could manifest an almost 50 percent increase in gift income over a single year.

Is it possible to double annual fund income in one year's time with an assertive fund raising program? Assertiveness is but one factor. The actual size of the goal is one major factor and another is the history of the development staff in following a sensitive plan of nurturing donor interest and upgrading gifts. The cultivation of donors is truly intuitive artistry, but the kind of artistry that pays dividends. The major concern has to be, Is there a giving vitality in the donor base? Are there sufficient donors who can be induced to increase their gifts?

Conditions within the organization must be capable of supporting such a major accomplishment. What conditions are required? In the case of the human services center, the annual fund program might have worked better had the board and the executive done advance long-range planning to define the fund raising mission, the goals, and the budget and to identify the constituency and prospects for solicitation. A high level of discipline is required in addition to a very high level of cooperation from members of the governing board and from the executive staff, the program staff, the support staff, the development committee of the board, and selected high-level volunteers as the solicitation task force. And, of course, prospective donors capable of giving major gifts must be available.

Constructing a Gift Range Chart

Let us reduce this planning for the human services center to a logical structure. What are the priorities? To begin with, the development officer should have constructed a gift range chart for the $55,000 annual fund goal. This critical planning process would have helped board members, the executive, and the financial committee chair to set a reasonable goal based on the hard evidence of recent gift experience as registered in the donor base. The chart determines the number of gifts at specific dollar levels required to attain a desired goal. It also defines the number of prospective donors that should be identified at each gift level to justify the projection that the goal will be reached (see Table 1.1).

A gift range chart is based on an equation forged by the experiences of past fund raising professionals. Such equations can be arithmetical projections for an annual or a capital fund program. The computations discussed here pertain to an annual fund program. The top 10 percent of the gifts shown to be required by the gift chart should produce 60 percent of the stated dollar goal. The next 20 percent of the gifts should produce the next 20 percent of

Table 1.1. Gift Range Chart for a $55,000 Annual Fund Program.

Gift Range	Number of Gifts	Number of Prospects	Cumulative Totals
$2,500	2	8 (4:1)	$5,000
2,000	3	12 (4:1)	11,000
1,500	8	24 (3:1)	23,000
1,000	10	30 (3:1)	33,000 (60%)
500	30	90 (3:1)	48,000
Below $500	Many from donor base		55,000

the goal. The final 70 percent of the gift should produce the rest of the money required to reach the goal. This equation is summarized in Table 1.2.

Moreover, the top two gifts should each equal 5 percent of the goal, to set the pattern of giving for other major donors.

Constructing gift range charts for both annual and capital programs will help the fund raising professional measure the scope of the task ahead because the chart computes the numbers and quality of gifts that will be required to reach the goal and the numbers of prospects that will have be identified at each gift level. At the conclusion of the program, the gift range chart becomes a useful evaluation tool for comparing performance against planning projections.

Without these hard data, fund raising planners will have a problem justifying any fund raising goal. "If only everyone will give $100" is not a valid projection. Asking people to "give your fair share" or "do your part" is not a valid technique for getting gifts of the required size.

Table 1.2. Annual Fund Gift Computations.

10% of the donors = 60% of the $	
20% of the donors = 20% of the $	
70% of the donors = 20% of the $	
100%	100%

Learning from the Donor Base

The history of fund raising supports the assumption that an organization new to the process will find it difficult, if not impossible, to double its annual fund income in the second or third year of its operation. The chances are quite strong that the new nonprofit organization (NPO) will not have developed a solid base of donors through the acquisition, renewal, and upgrading process. More attention to the sensitive process of donor cultivation and involvement will probably be required, and until an NPO has a dedicated base of regular donors willing to increase their gifts significantly, doubling the organization's income will be an unlikely feat.

For both old and new organizations, a donor base profile, a variation of the gift range chart, can be used periodically to test whether the donor base is enjoying good health or is suffering incipient pangs of debilitating lethargy. It is wise for development staff to profile the donor base every year because the exercise will produce a wealth of solid information that will serve the staff well, telling them not only about the health of the donor base but also whether it is or is not possible to increase annual fund production, launch a major gift program, or prepare for a large-goal capital program.

There is considerable wisdom in the donor base and within the files awaiting the attention of the development officer. Is current gift production advancing or is it hesitating, telegraphing problems ahead? To use the donor base for gift profiles, development officers must have names of donors and donors' continuing gift histories recorded in that base. Accordingly, information relating to the donors' interests, questions, and concerns and also information relating to accomplishments should be recorded. If your computer program does not permit this, change your program as fast as you can to one that does permit the recording of this precious data.

Every development office should have computer capability to record current gift data and to file it in a database that will preserve the information and be ready to report it back in various usable forms when required. Not too many years ago, this information was recorded on four-by-six-inch cards. Heaven help you if you have to do the same thing today. Instead, to profile your gift production, use the awesome facility of your computer to pull out data representing three years of gifts: the current year, the previous year, and the year before that (a basic version of this profile is shown on the next page in Table 1.3). Garner this information to test the vitality of your base and to update your knowledge about your most promising, most loyal donors, particularly those who might be considered prospects for major, special, or planned gifts. Ask yourself what should you know about these donors before you begin to blueprint your expanded annual fund for the year ahead or your plan for a major capital effort, or before you chart an exploratory effort to cultivate planned giving prospects.

The first inventory should be an update of the continuing gift patterns of current major donors, should there be any. Then some attention should be accorded to those who are not major donors yet but perhaps have the potential. They should be considered and researched as prospects for larger gifts.

Also examine whether the gift pattern is holding a steady profile, increasing, or declining. Table 1.3 illustrates a helpful donor base inventory to alert you to the presence of major gift prospects filed away in the depths of your computer records. Take a hard look at this particular information base at least twice a year. On the first go-through, record the raw numbers of gifts at each level. On the second round, substitute donor names for numbers, thus seeking names of possible major prospects.

Search for donors who repeat their gifts because this source represents a strength for the fund raising program. Search also for those who have increased their gifts in the most recent year, then for those who made their last gift in the previous year, and finally those who made their last gift three years ago. Is it not logical to conclude that the most recent repeating donors will be good prospects for someone to approach to ask for a major gift or, at least, an upgrade of the regular gift? After studying the donor base profile and coming to your own conclusions about the gift potential of the donor base, share that information with the development staff, then with the chief executive, and then with the development committee. If you are alert and subject to suggestion, you will find a host of ideas in your donor base to help you mount and maintain a creative program of donor cultivation and involvement.

**Table 1.3. Evaluating the Donor Base by Gift Levels:
$100 to $1,000 or More.**

Gift Level	Number in 1996	Number in 1995	Number in 1994
$1,000 or more			
750–999			
500–749			
250–499			
100–249			

Defining the Mission

Next among the priorities in fund raising is a defined statement of mission that reflects the dominant values of the organization and is a cogent argument as to why those values should be served, expanded, strengthened, and multiplied. This mission statement (as a part of the case statement) should give strong evidence throughout the annual fund period that the extra money is needed. Let it be accepted that it is difficult to raise significant money with an unfeeling case statement based on the simple principle that the organization needs the money for its budget. Need of money is an universal experience. The expression of that need will not excite any person, foundation, or corporation to double, triple, or quadruple a previous gift. The case for a significant gift increase has to be related to the mission and should make it clear why this particular mission should be served and how the programs to be funded can serve it.

Sifting through a stack of old releases and correspondence, I found a memorandum sent to his special friends by Harold Seymour, author of *Designs for Fund-Raising* (1966), a book that became a primer for fledgling fund raisers and a constant prod to older veterans. The memorandum focused on the case for a capital campaign and said, tersely, "Case must be copper bottomed and airtight." In other words, check and recheck your text. It must survive the most thorough critical scrutiny. It must appeal to the intellect. It must also stir the heart to induce the proper gift.

Conclusion

Readers may be asking whether the candidate for development officer at the human services center should have requested an opportunity to test the donor base as I have described in this chapter. Is it possible that she might have unearthed some strategic information that just possibly could have changed the executive's thinking about the best course to follow?

Some might say that such testing would be an unwarranted intrusion on the confidential records. Yet others who have actually followed this procedure, with the permission of the executive, have been able to garner critical data to guide the executive, the development committee, and the governing board to a realistic decision about the annual fund goal. It is not too difficult to change minds and to induce people to follow different paths, ones that hold greater promise for future development programs, when you can place hard evidence before decision makers to demonstrate that these paths are ones that will lead to desired results. Final fund raising goals should be based on the hard facts of the achievements of the past three years and on the ability to accumulate and nurture past donors, both internally and in the community, especially those who frequently commit major gifts to support the organization's mission.

Chapter Two

Growing a Successful Fund Raising Program

As a nonprofit organization evolves, it passes through three phases of fund raising: the beginning phase, the developing phase, and the maturing phase. Each phase reflects an advance in the process of attracting gift support from the nonprofit's constituency (see Figure 2.1). Moreover, different dynamics pertain in the three phases, and each commands a different quality of discipline and dedication from the development staff, executive team, and members of the governing board. Remember, as I have stated before, "Fund raising is a simple process but a demanding taskmaster."

Beginning: The First Phase

In the *beginning phase* of their fund raising experience, many nonprofits with limited staff and limited knowledge of the fund raising processes labor their way through fund raising growth. With sparse or no leadership resources, they work their way through various experiments, groping, testing, and often failing to reach their objectives.

They try valiantly; staff and volunteers work long hours in their endeavors to achieve the long-awaited success. However, the chances are that the lone staff fund raiser has limited experience, learned from reading pamphlets and attending an occasional workshop; that the executive and the financial officers know next to nothing about raising money, and that the members of the board disdain the process—"That's not why we joined your board." The young fund raiser tries desperately to raise funds, particularly

Figure 2.1. Three Phases of Fund Raising Growth.

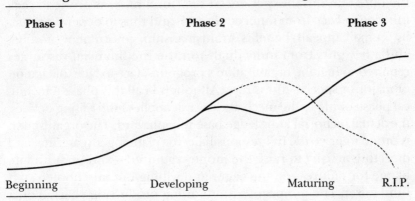

by staging a series of special events, conducting mailings, arranging door-to-door solicitations with youthful volunteers, and making personal visits to several foundations and corporations, without proper preparation and thus without much luck. The ultimate bountiful harvest of gifts from many sources continues to elude the organization.

This first phase is the technical, mechanical stage. The staff, the board, and the volunteers, if any, are prone to depend on random splinters of fund raising knowledge. They are not aware, for example, that fund raising special events rarely can support the budget needs of nonprofit organizations that lack an established constituency to help with these events and that lack boards that will assume the responsibility of planning, promoting, supporting, managing, and possibly financing the events. Fund raising events, or benefits as they are also called, return a value to nonprofits in terms of community exposure, volunteer involvement (sometimes quite reluctantly), and on occasion, a bit of money. They are not effective in the necessary development of a strong, active constituency that will remain loyal over the years and that will support ongoing programs by making consistent gifts to the annual fund.

In this initial, or testing phase, fund raising techniques are basic, dependent on "snippets" of information and not on truths that come from experience. The formative stage is the beginning of the development program's experience.

In many formative programs, there is no formal development officer, only a "staff fund raiser" who carries a heavy burden. During the time that this inexperienced staff fund raiser is prone to seek innocent advice from innocent friends and thus to depend primarily on mail appeals, benefits, grantsmanship, government funding, and a few gifts from individuals to raise the financial resources required to fuel the organization's programs, face-to-face solicitation of major or special gifts is rare. Although I call this phase a technical phase owing to the mechanical way it applies fund raising devices, the actual technical knowledge base is haphazard. The organization is prone to place the full responsibility for planning, organizing, and directing activity to raise the money required—and the ultimate blame for failure—on the eager and willing but unschooled staff fund raiser. The nonprofit's fund raising production charted on a progress growth scale (Figure 2.1) would reflect, understandably, a relatively flat progress curve. Some but not sufficient money is raised during these difficult initial years.

Phase 1, then, has many deficiencies. The fund raiser is considered to be a "vendor," one who holds certain technical skills but has little knowledge of professional fund raising. The fund raiser uses these technical, mechanical skills to "sell" the organization. The case for fund raising is primarily the fact that the organization needs money, needs it badly and, "By gosh, everybody should give. Give or our organization will have to stop doing good in service to the community." This is a down-to-earth basic budget appeal, a plain pitch to the guts, a sales appeal with no heart in it. It makes no reference to the human or societal needs that justify the existence of the nonprofit, no reference to its mission, its vision, and its program goals and objectives.

I have a four-by-four-inch card on my desk at home. It is a stark reminder that the case is the central element in the fund raising case, not the desperate need of budget money. Four words printed in black on the square white card plead for the tin cup: I NEED MONEY BAD! It is the shortest case I have ever read. It is, also, the most pitiful—it has no passion, no justification for the ask. A stark appeal based simply on the need for money does not touch too many hearts and, therefore, does not raise significant money. Yet this "begging" appeal is typical of the techniques used by inexperienced staff during the beginning phase. They use it because the concept of mission is not clear in their minds.

Developing: The Second Phase

When the fund raising program becomes more professional and more sensitive to human responses and to the requirements of individuals being solicited, the appeal moves away from basic budget needs. The case focus turns to the values inherent in the work of the organization, to the values of concern to the prospective donor, and to the human or societal needs of concern to the larger constituency.

At this point, the fund raising program is entering the *developing phase* as it becomes more aware of constituency responses and of the need to be open and as frank as possible in the presentation of the case and about the effectiveness of organizational programs and the organization's trustworthy management of financial and human resources.

The staff fund raiser becomes, or is replaced by, a director of development, who is provided with some basic staff. The development staff are charged to design and implement a forward-looking fund raising plan that will generate the annual, capital, and special gift dollars essential to meet program needs. The fund raising progress chart (Figure 2.1) reflects some energy with an upward move in its curve. Encouraging progress is being made. Staff members are asserting themselves to put the principles and techniques of fund raising to work. Efforts are being made to expand the donor base and to involve volunteers in the solicitations.

In the developing phase, the executive staff and the members of the governing board begin to assume some of the responsibility for activating and evaluating the fund raising plan that they approved. A development committee is formed, although it typically lacks the dynamism of leaders who are willing both to give and to ask for gifts. Members prefer to serve on an advisory body, with the definition of their task limited to the review, possible modification, and final approval of the fund raising plan. At this stage, however, the development committee does deliberate the necessity of embarking on a planned giving plan. Several presentations on the value of both a major gift and planned giving plan are usually placed before the committee. Yet committee members typically remain in a contemplative mode (much to the development officer's chagrin), suspecting that if they approve this concept, they will have to come to a decision on their position about giving and getting.

Programs approved for fund raising by the development director and the development committee use direct mail for acquisition and gift renewal purposes, first-class mailings for gift upgrading, and a judicious number of special events. In addition, the fund raising agenda includes solicitation of special purpose gifts from individuals, foundations, and corporations. This mix offers abundant opportunities for generating financial resources to support operating programs.

Too many nonprofits in this phase depend upon the development officer and development staff to assume full responsibility for all aspects of the development program. Minimum developmental support is sought from but not provided by the chief executive, program and support staff, and board members. At this stage, the organization does not realize its full resources development capability. If it does not grow beyond this stage, it will never reach its full capability.

Thus, phase 2 also has a number of deficiencies. The development program is primarily staff centered. The board members appear reluctant to offer their support. Some do but not many. Executive, program, and administrative staff, for the most part, are supporting this important endeavor. A good deal of creative energy and a good many valuable linkages to prospective major gift donors are being denied to the development staff and, therefore, opportunities to invite major donors to associate themselves with the organization are being bypassed.

The development officer's task is to overcome these deficiencies, to induce trustees and the executive team to commit themselves to support the development program. At this point, the development officer must view himself or herself as a teacher-trainer and must launch a thoughtfully constructed training program to educate the executive team, the program heads, and the members of the board in the principles and techniques of fund raising. A complicated task, yes; but once it is done, the pace of activity will accelerate, and greater funds will be raised. During the developing phase, the development officer takes the role of facilitator. In this role, he or she can serve as a mediating force, negotiating with key leaders, staff, board members, and the larger community to attract additional leadership energy to the development program. An infusion of energy is required in the form of more linkages to key community leaders and to potential major gift prospects, to individuals with the pulling power to induce others to commit themselves as givers and as solicitors.

This development program is beginning to mature. As a maturing program, it must be able to attract that precious quality of leadership that will make a difference in the production of large gifts. The development person now focuses energy on identification, recruitment, and relationship maintenance with a quality of leadership that will make a difference in the development program. The development officer's human relations skills are being honed. This person must understand that first priority in the development program must be to identify, develop, and maintain relationships with key people in a position to change the course of the fund raising program from lethargic and inconsistent progress to progress toward the heights on the growth chart. As the growth moves up in an encouraging form, volunteer leaders will be bringing in larger and larger gifts. This is fund raising.

Maturing: The Third Phase

In the *maturing stage,* all things come together in good style. Maximum use is being made of the leadership resources readily offered by trustees, executive staff, program and support staff, and volunteers. A well-schooled development officer is the program choreographer, directing the various staff members and volunteers, integrating them into the plan, and blending people's unique talents into a working entity. The focus at this stage is always on the vision and the mission of the organization.

The professional development officer, now a skilled strategist, can expect expanding help from the leadership in searching out and qualifying prospective donors. Research into prospect ranks will be intensified to produce precious hints about linkages to large gift prospects. Help will be available to identify and activate creative staff and volunteer talent. The skills bank—researching, writing, establishing prospect relations, developing and soliciting prospects—will be enhanced. Staff and volunteers will be willing to put their skills and their energy to work to move the program to success. Fund raising becomes exciting and, therefore, more productive, because it employs the institution's full capacity for creative thinking and takes advantage of its strong presence in and its powerful outreach to the community.

In this stage, the progress growth chart (Figure 2.1) displays a rising scale splitting to form two branches, one a solid line rising confidently to greater fund raising accomplishments and the other a broken line descending sharply to an unfortunate target marked R.I.P., "rest in peace." The split defines a determining moment in the progression of fund raising activity, when it can continue to soar to new heights or decline to the degree that it will not be able to produce the financial resources required to fuel the tanks of the ongoing programs.

What can make it soar to the heights? A continuing energetic program that reaches to the outer boundaries of the organization's stakeholders. Efforts must be made to assure stakeholders' continuing allegiance to the organization and to its mission. The development officer's focus must be at all times on major gifts from individuals and what it takes to secure those crucial gifts. People's giving is certainly the primary priority. Corporations, foundations, associations, and other organizations are the second priority. Leadership must be at the core of this priority. There can be no dissipation of volunteer energy and diminution of commitment to the cause of fund raising on the part of the executive and development teams.

In this stage, the chief development officer must be a skilled strategist, a person able to look around the corners of destiny. The board members must be alerted to the requirements of the fund raising process and be made aware of their responsibilities as trustees, as primary stewards of the nonprofit.

Fund raising strategies have no energy of their own. Strategies must be activated to release energy. Growth is less in phases 1 and 2 than in phase 3 because mechanical lackluster devices are used to attract few and very small gifts. There are no magnets in these devices to pull other than minimum gifts in the direction of the nonprofit. The motivational pull to give is not there. And if the first- and second-stage nonprofits do not learn how to diversify their fund raising by involving the executive team, the trustees, and other key volunteers to search out and to promote major gifts, what kind of future are they facing? If one of their major funders— a foundation, corporation, or government—withdraws its funding, how long will the nonprofit lacking both a broad donor base and fund raising experience last? Without a well-cultivated donor base with major gift experience, what steps can the nonprofit take to compensate for the loss of one or more major grants? There is also an irony here. In the long term, the nonprofit can make some corrections, but can it wait that long? In the short term, the pressure to raise budget money is too severe, the obstacles too great.

Now, this situation can pertain to the third-stage, the maturing phase nonprofit, also. How can this possibly happen? It happens through careless management, through disdain for the fact that fund raising may be a simple process but a demanding taskmaster, through taking trustees and key volunteers for granted and not acknowledging their precious gifts of time and talent. It also comes from not sending thank-you letters to donors within twenty-four to forty-eight hours, misspelling volunteers' and donors' names, and not sending a financial report when a donor requests it. These and other adventures in careless behavior tend to persuade donors to direct their gifts to more responsive, more attentive organizations. Eschew carelessness.

Beware of high tech. Never disregard its working partner, high touch! Donors are too precious to disregard. The computer is a remarkable instrument, facilitating a variety of procedures that can bring life to the work of the development staff. Treat it properly, and it will be a blessing to the development processors. Treat it carelessly, and it will bite back by offending donors—names misspelled, wrong first names used, and gifts of $250 or more not recorded in an acknowledgment letter mailed to the donor within the time constraints dictated by IRS requirements. These and many other tricks will bite careless processors. Watch for them.

And do not forget that there are many times when the telephone can be used for a warm thank-you call to the donor who does not expect it at the precious instant that you receive that donor's unanticipated gift. Try this particularly when you are tired or depressed for some reason or other. The emotional lift you will experience after the call is completed is unbelievable.

As a strategist, the chief development officer in the maturing phase has a helicopter view of the organization, fully understanding the intention, the meaning and the drive, and the purpose of the mission statement and its implication for service program execution and for the fund raising program. As a strategist, the chief development officer is also an active and respected member of the nonprofit's management team. His or her primary responsibility is to search out, recruit, nurture, and maintain continuing relations with strategic partners, those volunteer leaders who "are the creative citizens, with what Harry Emerson Fosdick has called 'a sense of privilege.' They light the way, originate action, take the responsibility, establish the standards, create the confidence, sustain the mood, and keep things moving" (Seymour, 1966, p. 4). Strategic partners understand their role without being told. Their sights are always on the major gifts that will set a giving pattern to ensure the success of every fund raising undertaking.

It is not unusual for the chief executive, chair of the development committee, trustees, and key staff persons, as well as donors and prospective donors, to seek the chief development officer's guidance on important issues. At this stage, he or she can serve as an internal consultant to the organization. The chief development officer also functions as a boundary spanner, maintaining intelligence contact with the organization's constituency domain. Competition will require it; changing forces in the environment will compel it. The chief development officer will be a major force in the day-to-day life of a successful nonprofit organization, helping guide it to its destiny in service to society.

A Bumpy Road

Nonprofits occasionally encounter difficult periods when things tend to fall apart. It is rare to float comfortably from beginning to developing to maturing phases in a straightforward sequence. It seems that a nonprofit has to stop periodically to pay some sort of advancement toll. It jumps joyfully from the beginning to the developing phase only to experience the agony of a setback.

After a recovery, it finds itself at the top of the maturing phase for a glorious period. Then the mail returns falter and, coincidentally, it loses several key givers. The progression from beginning to developing seems to be haphazard, but that is inevitable. (How often can Mr. Murphy be right? Quite often, it seems.) For this reason, the development staff should conduct periodical informal program audits, taking a pulse or performing an EKG to test whether or not the development program is healthy.

Whether your organization is in phase 1, phase 2, or phase 3, it is wise to take stock of the health of your donor base (some methods of doing this are described in Chapter One). What is happening while you are slaving away to meet your production expectations? Are you adding new donors? Equally important, are you losing any regular donors? Are you maintaining the level of renewals? Is the percentage of upgrades remaining steady? Are you able to encourage upgrades by inviting special gifts from your regular donors? How often do you have a telephone conversation with donors who upgrade regularly?

Conclusion

As your organization progresses through the phases of fund raising development, stay alert throughout. Keep in touch with the state of your program. Grab the precious moment when success is in sight. Make the most out of that moment, to achieve the goal so important to the fate of the organization. Strive always to reach the ultimate maturing phase. But remember that periodically you can slip to phase 1 and have to start all over again.

Chapter Three

Developing Leadership for Fund Raising

Leaders—staff and volunteers in fund raising—play an important role: inspiring and directing, serving as a role model in giving and getting. Therefore, an analysis of the role of leadership in effective fund raising is in order.

A number of people have investigated the leadership traits important in nonprofit organizations. For example, the late Carolyn Charles, an honored faculty member of The Fund Raising School from 1975 to 1977, spoke much truth when she told her classes:

> There are many traits in a community leader, but only one essential, i.e., that much abused and ill-defined word "charisma." There are, of course, many other desirable qualities: style, responsibility, good humor, decency, knowledge of the organization's purpose and current situations, respect of the community, sensitivity, courage (fund raising is not the place for the weak in recovery power), persistence, optimism, public speaking ability, and willingness to give and willingness to ask others to give. Not to mention a capacity for the long view, the perspective on the nonprofit's present and future goals (excessive attention to detail is the opium of the not quite successful leader). But hardly anybody has more than a few of these qualities [1974, p. 81].

Peter Drucker, in the foreword to *The Leader of the Future,* takes a different position on the value of charisma in his discussion of the traits of leaders: "The one and only *personality trait* the effective ones I have encountered did have in common was something that they did *not* have: they had little or no 'charisma,' and little use either for the term or for what it signifies" (Hesselbein, Goldsmith, and Beckhard, 1996, p. xii).

Robert Greenleaf has yet another view of leadership traits, finding that different ones distinguish various forms of leadership. A strong advocate of servant leadership, a concept that he brought to life through his writings and teachings (for example, Greenleaf, 1991), he believed that servant leadership tends to draw allegiance from others in response to the clear servant status of the leader. The best leader, in his view, is the one who leads not from power but from a primary motivation to serve. Thus, the leader who begins with a genuine desire to serve others is the one who demonstrates sterling qualities of leadership.

A variety of people have posed a variety of nonprofit leadership traits, all appropriate. What I want to emphasize here, however, is the vital importance of the presence of what followers recognize as leadership, because that recognized leadership is a critical element in the implementation of effective fund raising. Veterans of major campaigns are consistent in their assertion that the right leadership is a strategic value that ensures the success of any fund raising activity. Yes, they will agree that a convincing case statement adds drama to the presentation of the cause needing funding support. Yes, they will admit, the human and societal needs stated in the institution's mission statement must be valid, thoughtfully catalogued, and attested to by authorities to give credence to the appeal. Yes, the fund raising plan must give evidence that discipline will be the glue that will hold the campaign structure together during the difficult months of strategic maneuvering to attain the goal. These are the major factors, along with the availability of sufficient valid major gift prospects, that are crucial to the success of the program, but they will stand for naught if there is no qualified, inspired leadership team available at the helm of the intensive annual fund or the drawn-out complicated capital campaign to guide it to its goal.

Without this leadership, the fund raising effort will limp painfully to a bleak conclusion, despite Herculean efforts on the part of the development officer and development staff to press the activity to a successful end. The proper person, with the proper spirit and the proper contacts and with the proper philosophy about the propriety and importance of gifts as investments serving the public good, makes a significant difference in the final fund raising accomplishment.

The rest of this chapter examines where this leadership responsibility should reside. Should it be relegated solely to the governing board, to the executive team, to the volunteer development committee, or to the development staff? Or should there be a leadership partnership, involving each of these entities and possibly key representatives of the program staff, to forge an impressive center of creative energy that will get the development program off the ground and drive the development program forward to success? I believe that the leadership partnership is essential.

Candidates for Leadership

Prospects for fund raising leadership can be found on the governing board, in listings of past board members, among the members of the development committee, possibly among community leaders and the more prominent major donors, and at times, among individuals that the organization is serving.

The development director should maintain a file for each candidate, with notes about interests, reasons for association with the organization, and possible willingness to give. The director would be wise to conduct continuing research in the community to select at least three to five primary candidates who might qualify to assume the leadership mantle for any upcoming campaign. Ideally and logically, this candidate should be drawn from the board of trustees—a reality that should be kept in mind by the chief executive and the chair of the board when selecting prospective board members and conducting trustee orientation sessions or annual planning retreats. If this eventuality has not been foreseen, then even though the board discusses and approves each major fund raising effort, when a move is made to select a general chair for that effort, board candidates will typically be absent. At this point, the development officer, the development committee, and the chief executive must apply themselves to the selection and the enlistment of a community leader to head the fund raising effort.

Of course, planning for fund raising leadership should not be left to the final moments, weeks, or even months before the program is launched. The internal leadership should accept the hard fact that top-level leadership in a major campaign is a requisite. It should be made clear to trustees that securing financial resources through the gift-making process should be a priority responsibility of the primary stewards of the organization, the trustees themselves. Members of the governing board bear the responsibility of approving all financial transactions and, as a consequence, they should also bear the duty of determining how financial resources can be secured and how they themselves can be involved in the process. Beyond this determination, trustees should be part of the action to acquire the resources. In short, they should be willing to play a major role in fund raising.

When a board member is not available as a fund raising program leader, is it worth the time to search out, recruit, and train volunteer leaders, and is it worth the investment to retain a consultant to plan and direct the program as its professional leader? These questions are generally asked by young, relatively inexperienced executive officers who are trying to save money by not retaining a professional, and by eager sophomore development officers who are trying to make their mark by planning and directing a major capital program without the help of a community leader. I have been challenged by such persons as to the accuracy of my contention that appropriate leadership is essential. "Why is volunteer leadership so important to the successful outcome of this campaign?" a development officer has asked. "Why can't I do this by myself? I have had the experience. Why should I waste valuable time and money trying to find, to enlist, to train, and then to supervise volunteers who always have their own ideas about how it should be done? All of this takes time. It requires an expenditure of precious creative energy. I can use that energy to get started with my solicitations. What's the big deal? What can volunteers do that I cannot do by myself? [Or the chief executive and I together can put this show on the road.] And what's this about a consultant as a professional leader? Wasted money!" Fortunately these people changed their minds after reading the findings and conclusions of a feasibility study stating that without top-level leadership, volunteer and professional, the campaign would fail to meet its mark.

The Primary Team

The primary leadership team for all fund raising activity should include the development officer, the chief executive, the board chair, development committee members, the enlisted volunteer campaign chair, and in the case of a major program, a professional fund raising consultant. The volunteer fund raising chair and the consultant are critical forces when a nonprofit is considering embarking on a major effort. The energy, skills, and enthusiasm that can be provided by a well-known enthusiastic volunteer leader as fund raising chair will energize and strengthen the internal team. A qualified professional consultant will be an asset that helps guide the team to goal achievement.

Strategic Value of Volunteers

What volunteers are required? It is essential to have a dedicated, qualified volunteer leader and sufficient competent volunteer solicitors who know and understand the market and who will devote quality time to asking the right person for the right gift for the right program at the right time. If the volunteer leader is of prominent stature in the community, that standing by itself can be sufficient to validate the program and to call to the fore the interest and support of other strategically important volunteers and contributors to fill the ranks of program workers and solicitors. With these committed volunteers on hand, the successful conclusion of a fund raising program can be a singular fund raising benefit.

It is difficult to exaggerate the impact that nonprofit leadership can acquire by drawing other known leaders into the fund raising fold. It is a basic truth that the right community leaders can open doors that might otherwise be closed to professional staff, including the development officer and the chief executive. Access to the persons behind these doors has the potential to change the course of a campaign from sad failure to joyful success. The right volunteer leaders who can ask the right person to make the right gift make the difference between an exciting effort soaring to achieve the goal and an abject failure celebrated only by endless exchanges of blame.

Volunteer leadership makes a difference by serving as a conduit to individuals capable of giving pacesetting gifts. These gifts act like a magnet, attracting other important contributions. Moreover, the commitment and enthusiasm of respected individuals can be contagious, a relentless pull that draws other leaders to join the program as major givers and as willing, effective solicitors. The resulting surge of energy will tend to lift the adrenaline level of any program. Every once in a while, the tanks of any campaign must be refueled. A new addition of high-caliber leadership to the ranks at strategic moments can infuse high octane energy into the tanks of the campaign team, making things happen again.

Seymour points out that "in any field of human activity, not just in fund-raising, the leaders are indeed rare—never more than 5 per cent of any group or constituency, and usually less." And, as mentioned in the last chapter, Seymour goes on to call volunteer leaders "the creative citizens, with what Harry Emerson Fosdick has called 'a sense of privilege.' They light the way, originate action, take the responsibility, establish the standards, create the confidence, sustain the mood, and keep things moving" (1966, p. 4).

Yes, indeed, these are key volunteers, gems that will drive your program to success. A member of the fund raising profession should never naïvely assume that he or she alone is sufficient to plan, direct, and drive a major campaign to a fruitful harvest without the inspired motivation and the involvement of these supportive "creative citizens." Again, in Seymour's sage words, "when the people are with you and are giving your cause their attention, interest, confidence, advocacy, and service, financial support should just about take care of itself. Whereas without them—in the right quality and quantity, in the right places, and the right states of mind and spirit—you might as well go and get lost. So you'd better know as much about people as you can, keep it ever in mind, and always let it light your way" (p. ix). Never has it been said better!

Setting the Stage for Leadership

There are certain concerns that should be deliberated when planning the structure of a team to lead the fund raising program. The first concern is that fund raising has never won any national honors as the most popular indoor or outdoor sport. As a matter of fact, many people tend to view fund raising with some disdain, not truly conferring on the art form the respect it merits and has earned over the millennia. This disdain insinuates itself into the planning process, complicating the enrollment of a competent, functioning volunteer team.

Perhaps fund raising is so maligned because it was once synonymous with charity and charity was considered to be begging, thus the term "beggars" for early fund raising solicitors. We elders, generally tabbed as the "old walruses" of the profession, dream of that wonderful day when a young person, boy or girl, perhaps ten, twelve, or fourteen years of age, will approach a parent, serious of mien, hesitant in speech, but yet determined to give voice to that majestic dream that he or she has been repressing: "Mom, Dad, I have given serious thought to this dream. Please don't worry about me; please don't laugh. This is my life desire. When I grow up, truly, truly, I want to be a fund raiser. Please don't laugh; please believe. Embrace me and help me start on the road to the realization of that wonderful dream! Please!"

Let it be said that fund raising is a relatively simple yet fascinating and fully engrossing human endeavor. However, the very fact that many people see it as demeaning will cause them to shy away from any association with fund raising—rejecting any invitation to become a volunteer leader or a donor. Sometimes, they will even reject an offer to become a paid professional practitioner.

The fund raising practitioner must be aware of these nuisance barriers. She or he must prepare a thoughtful enlistment strategy based on serious research, learning as much as possible about each potential leadership candidate's interests, values, and also past volunteer experience, that is, the person's willingness to serve the public good through gifts of time, talent, and treasure. Candidate familiarity with the organization, its mission, its goals, its programs, and its vision is absolutely essential. This information, along with the candidate's gift history, should be on file in the development database.

The second concern is the readiness of the organization itself to cope with such a time-demanding task as a major annual fund program or a capital campaign. Will non–fund raising staff be willing and able to work in empathy with volunteer leadership? Will a support system be in place to foster the working partnerships so essential to the success of the campaign? Will staff accept the additions to their workload necessitated by campaign pressures? Is leadership available within the organization, from the board or from the staff? Will it manifest itself in the fund raising activity? Will it cooperate with enlisted community leadership? Are board and staff members prepared to make their own gifts? Is the concept of voluntary fund raising safely ensconced within the culture of the organization? Will that institutional culture pleasantly accept and support volunteer leadership for its fund raising programs? If board members resist accepting leadership responsibilities, how will the organization explain the fact that its trustees are not making themselves available for leadership responsibilities?

Nonprofits, for the most part, are accepting the reality that an inside team must be constituted as a continuing focal point for the fund raising operation if fund raising is to be responsive to the organization's diverse and continuing financial needs.

Team building within the organization is an essential act if appropriate energy and attention are to be dedicated to the overall fund raising process, and if that process is to be accorded the dignity and respect required for productive accomplishment. Four inside individuals integral to the team are the chief executive officer, the chair or president of the board, the chief development officer, and the development committee chair. Why these specific people? Because they serve in pivotal sensitive posts where they can either support or block productive fund raising action.

The Chief Executive Officer

In particular, the support and approval of the chief executive officer is an absolute requirement. Such support and approval encourages progress; lack of support and approval inhibits progress. The position of the chief executive is sufficiently authoritative that she or he can prod individuals into action through simple persuasion and by serving as a role model, by assuring full cooperation, by encouraging, and by explaining how important people's service will be to the organization. However, if the chief executive should abhor fund raising and resist any involvement with it, that negative energy will convey itself to others in the organization and dissuade many from making any significant contribution in dollars or time.

A leader without followers is an empty vessel. The true role of leadership—board and staff—is giving people the kind of support that they will need to succeed. Motivation must start at the top and then trickle down to teach, and then to touch and inspire, each member of the staff. Support must start with the management team. Nothing is more debilitating than a cold stare from the executive team and program staff members when the subject of fund raising is placed on the table for discussion. I recall a hospital fund raising program during which the following horror story took place. The chief executive sat unmoving in his office, opposite the office where volunteers and fund raising leaders were meeting to prepare a plan. He never said hello, nor did he step into the office to express his gratitude or to offer help or guidance. The volunteer chair of the program asked several times, "When is Bozo going to join us?" It was up to me to bolster the team members' spirits and to keep the fund raising planning on target. We surpassed the goal despite the executive's rude demeanor.

A cold stare, an unbearable moment of silence, eyes avoiding contact, a building uneasiness in the room effectively and efficiently put to rest any further discussion on the subject of support for an upcoming fund raising campaign. But one lingering, pesky question must be asked by the shattered development officer, even when he or she suspects what the answer will be: "But how do we plan to staff and conduct this campaign?" The chief executive's soul-smashing response is often, "But isn't that why we hired you?"

This is a dreadfully unkind, unfair, energy-sapping, brain-numbing, heart-stopping, responsibility-dodging response. In it, there is no demonstration of leadership by the person who primarily represents the mission, the vision, and the spirit of the organization. This answer communicates the executive staff's lack of basic understanding of the fund raising process. It is particularly foolhardy to ask the development staff to manage an ongoing fund raising program and, at the same time, to manage a full-fledged capital campaign. These are not compatible assignments. Each exercises a considerable pull on the energy resources of the staff persons involved. A person with limited experience in fund raising would have a miserable time planning and directing a complicated program such as a capital campaign or an annual fund. There are times when one can lead, and times when one can barely follow.

It is a puzzle to me that although many books are being written about nonprofit management, board responsibilities, and the role of the executive staff, very few of these books put a spotlight on or offer any counseling about the responsibility of trustees, executive teams, and program staff in the fund raising process as planners, as givers, and as solicitors of major and pacesetting gifts. These individuals should be members of the fund raising team and any writer on the subject of nonprofit management should not duck this critical subject.

How often during board retreats and how often during board meetings do the trustees and executive team members candidly discuss the matter of fund raising and their stewardship? Who is willing to open this subject to candid discussion of what stewardship means in terms of those willing to lead, those who want to follow, and those who really desire to disappear into the dust? It is a refreshing experience to hear a board chair testify to the importance of trustees' involvement in fund raising. It is even more refreshing to witness board members soliciting each other face to face, in an effort to upgrade annual giving by trustees. Solicitation of trustees and key staff by mail is an empty gesture. So is the announcement during a meeting prior to a campaign that this is the time for trustees to give. It is worth repeating that trustees should understand that leaders without followers are not leaders.

The chief executive's endorsement of a major fund raising campaign is a requisite. The executive is the lengthened shadow of the nonprofit organization. Her or his negative reaction to assuming fund raising leadership assignments will sound the death knell for any fund raising program, permitting board members and staff also to separate themselves from the task. Although the chief executive cannot assume direction of the intensive fund raising plan—because she or he is preoccupied with management and board tasks such as financial overview and stewardship, staff support, and program overview—the chief executive absolutely must carry the flag for fund raising by giving generously at the beginning of the program and accepting strategic solicitation assignments whenever an executive presence will make a difference.

The responsibility for fund raising management is properly delegated to a competent development officer. This professional, however, must be able to depend on the full support of the executive team, members of the board, and program support staff whenever required. This officer should have the privilege of retaining outside professional consultants to assist with the campaign. And as described earlier, the leadership of a highly respected community figure to serve as campaign chair and to work in close partnership with the development officer or with a professional fund raising consultant is also crucial to the success of a major campaign.

In short, saying, "but that is why we hired you" in reaction to a development officer's question about board and executive assistance in planning and staffing a campaign is a thoughtless response to a serious question.

The Chair of the Board

Cyril O. Houle elegantly characterizes the "primary task" of the board chair as "helping diverse personalities merge into an effective 'social whole'" (1960, p. 11). The forging of the interests, talents, and energies of board members into a workable "social whole" immediately before the launching of a major fund raising program must be accepted as yeoman service, an accomplishment that should have an impressive impact on the organization's ability to generate much needed financial resources for decades into the future.

The chair of the board of trustees is the primary steward of the board. He or she is in a strategic position to meld the trustees into a creative whole and to show them how to invest themselves and to encourage others to invest themselves and their available resources in support of critical actions that will generate the financial resources required for the organization's operating programs. The board of trustees, merged into a force dedicated to the continuing advancement of the social whole, can serve as a powerful tool to enlist the philanthropic support of the larger community.

If the board chair and the chief executive share the belief that positive fund raising can make a difference in the continuing good health and advancement of the organization, they need to alert each trustee to that fact. By expressing their enthusiasm, conviction, and commitment, they can extend their spirit, inducing other trustees to become a part of the fund raising team. In this manner, the "social whole" can have a significant influence on the organization's capacity to raise much-needed funds.

Again, in the wise words of Houle, "It is the chairman's task to lead and to restrain, to blend in proper proportion the more capable and vocal members with the less experienced and silent ones. It is his/her job to foster such a unity of purpose and such a loyalty to objectives that each individual realizes that his/her own judgment is a part of the collective wisdom of the board" (1960, p. 11). Can it be that Houle is describing a wholehearted entry of trustees into the practice and support of the joyful celebration of fund raising? Perhaps it is a dream, but what a blessing that would be.

This unity, this allegiance to the mission, this acceptance of the torch of accountability is the expression of the "social whole" as it must be articulated by the board chair to shape the board into a productive entity. The board chair's role in this regard recalls Greenleaf's description (1991) of the prototypical servant leader:

> The servant leader is servant first. It begins with the natural feeling that one wants to serve, to serve first. Then conscious choice brings one to aspire to lead. The difference manifests itself in the care taken by the servant—first to make sure that other people's highest priority needs are being served. The best test, and difficult to administer, is: "Do those served grow as persons, becoming healthier, wiser, freer, more autonomous, more likely themselves to become servant leaders? And what is the effect on the least privileged in society, will they benefit, or at least, not be further deprived?" [p. 7].

James P. Shannon, former executive director of the General Mills Foundation, believes that shared power is power multiplied—you can give it away and still get more of it back. He also believes that the best trustees are humble enough to know that they can improve. Can we practitioners change trustees, ourselves, and in the process the world around us?

The Development Officer

The development officer, as the pivotal person in the total development process, is primarily a teacher and a manager; thus, she or he is a leader, a planner, an advocate for the cause, a communicator, a negotiator, an analyst, a cheerleader, an activist, a boundary spanner, and a bouncer of multiple balls to keep the fund raising action synchronized, spirited, and moving forward. This person is the staff professional whose job it is to manage all aspects of the ongoing fund raising program. She or he reports to the chief executive and through the executive to the governing board. Throughout, the development officer works in harmony with the board development committee and coordinates all fund raising plans with the chair and committee members and, of course, with the chief executive.

The Chair of the Development Committee

The development committee is usually commissioned by the board. Therefore, it should be a standing committee of the board. The board chair selects and appoints the committee chair. In most responsible nonprofits with workable development programs, the development officer and the chief executive also have a say in the selection of the most able committee leader. Obviously, it is essential for the development officer to have a part in this selection, because the committee chair and the development officer will have to work together and in harmony with the committee to achieve the annual fund and special fund raising goals of the organization.

What the Team Must Understand

The value of the fund raising process and the need for compatibility among team members are sensitive qualities to convey to every person on the internal fund raising team. This team, working in harmony, can stir the entire organization to action. In addition, an awareness that fund raising can be a demanding taskmaster can stand the team in good stead during difficult periods.

These are harsh realities that must be understood and addressed. If the team is to pose itself as a fund raising partnership, a functioning force to ensure the continuing supply of financial and human capital to fuel the nonprofit's engines, the partners must respect each other. They must cooperate with each other and commit themselves to give substance to their service to the mission and goals of the organization.

Finally, consultant Gary Wolff offers these words of good sense on the leadership team concerns that hover constantly over our work:

> Executive directors, members of governing boards, key program executives of the organization and others are not commonly aware of the multiple-faceted complex journey that must be undertaken for fund raising success. They may have very limited knowledge and/or interest, or they possess bits of information, just enough to help confuse, diffuse or refuse the best thinking and planning possible by a development professional.

> Development people often lack the depth of skill-awareness, personal confidence to adhere to proven methods and/or the commitment to serve the constituency of the cause, not only the professional leadership. This involves continuous teachings by the development officer directed to the CEO, the trustees, the fellow staff members, volunteer and donors.

> This means possessing the rooted stance (granted or attained) on the executive staff team and the respect that will manifest attention and creditability for the fund raising principles that are shared, plans that are proposed and action steps that are to be conducted [personal communication, 1995].

Conclusion

Development officers deserve to ask for and receive recognition as critical members of nonprofit management teams. Often that position of influence is not acknowledged when executives and trustees are visioning an organization's future and charting its course.

Development professionals who have been given significant responsibility for fund raising success and appropriate opportunity to participate in management decision making will, from day one, be better prepared to request the development role description needed to accomplish the business at hand. Orchestration of a variety of educational exercises by the development professional will help all involved to understand and accept the importance of fund raising leadership and what is needed for maximum results.

Moreover, the chief development officer should be permitted the privilege of attending all board meetings, except when confidential matters are being discussed.

If the chief development officer is functioning in accordance with the requirements of this leadership position, she or he is performing as a boundary scanner, as a communication conduit to the extremities of the nonprofit's constituency environment. In this role, the development chief is fulfilling a precious function, maintaining a positive communication link with constituents far and near. It is essential for this person to be sensitive to and knowledgeable about every aspect of the nonprofit's governance, management, and program policies and procedures in order to maintain communication integrity between the nonprofit and its broad-flung constituency.

Chapter Four

The Art of Asking with Composure

The first time that I asked for a gift—it was for an independent secondary school, decades ago—I found it fairly easy to talk about the school, its educational program, and its many accomplishments. But when the prospect asked the critical question, "What are you seeking?" I lost my composure. I found it difficult to ask for the suggested amount of $100. The prospective donor evidently sensed my uneasiness, so he set the amount for me, asking quietly, "Will $500 do?" In the matter of a few seconds, I learned an important lesson. At strategic moments in a solicitation, silence can be a virtue. Never again did I lose my composure, but I did make practiced use of judicious silence during the period of the ask quite frequently. I learned also that the solicitation focus should be more on the case than on dollars or on mechanical aspects of solicitation. This has been my creed since.

Understanding Giving

Keep in mind always that giving is more the dictate of the heart than the command of the brain. The mind may reluctantly say, "Well, all right, we should give something." The heart will counter with, "Come, come, it is not nearly enough." In every solicitation, wrap yourself in your mission. If you are preparing to enter a home or a business or foundation office and feel unsure of yourself, just step aside and let your mission do the talking for you. Or if you prefer, think of what you need to do in the terms used by a member of a Fund Raising School class in Mexico, "Kick yourself aside and give your mission the right of way."

All the principles of fund raising must come to a critical focus sharpened by the reality of the case, not dulled by the corrosive forces of procrastination. Whether we are approaching governments, foundations, corporations, service clubs, or individuals, these principles point to a basic truth in nonprofit work: today, somebody has to ask somebody for some money. That is the process of solicitation, and solicitation requires asking for money, or stock certificates, or real estate, or something else of substance.

For many people, the solicitation is a harsh exercise in agony, something to be avoided at all times. That is why many volunteers and even staff persons will promise to take on other chores in an effort to avoid the task of asking someone for money. A woman, an executive of a remarkable program involving nineteen children, fifteen of them adopted, explained her reticence about solicitation this way: "We have nineteen children in this house. We have nine bathrooms to serve them. I am willing to clean each of those bathrooms every day rather than take on the dreadful task of asking one person to give me money!" Obviously some hate to solicit. However, others will truly enjoy the experience.

Two working philosophies have guided me through my more than four decades in the fund raising profession:

Philosophy 1. People need and want to give, yet many do not know how, or to whom, or how much to give. A visit by an ethical experienced fund raising professional or dedicated volunteer is a service, not an imposition, giving the person the privilege of a decision. In every solicitation, there is either a yes or a no or, occasionally, a maybe. We should not usurp anyone's privilege of saying either yes or no. That privilege belongs to the prospect. If we do not exert ourselves to visit with the prospect, even when we anticipate a no, that person will never have the opportunity to enjoy the privilege of saying yes.

We often do anticipate a no. We agonize over the asking because we are absolutely sure that the prospect will say no, and we will be devastated. Accordingly, we say no for the prospect by not asking. But when we do this, we deny the prospect the opportunity to show appreciation or to demonstrate his or her caring for the exemplary work of nonprofit organizations. It is amazing how many times a no has been converted into a yes through gentle conversation, patient listening, and soft persuasion. So many times, a no is simply an introduction to a delayed yes.

Philosophy 2. Pressure or intimidation should never play a role in the solicitation process. Philanthropic giving to serve the public good is every person's entitlement. It should always be a freely willed action. People should be able to give according to their means, their own interests, and their own inclinations, without pressure. The decision should always be theirs.

At The Fund Raising School, we devote several hours to both a discussion and a testing of the concept of solicitation. The class starts with a brainstorming exercise designed to find answers to three important questions: Why do people give?, Why don't people give?, and Why don't people like to ask for money? The responses are fascinating and revealing.

Why Do People Give?

If people were to be asked why they give to a nonprofit, the fund raising students said these were the kinds of answers they would generally give: "I want to support the mission of the organization," "I approve of the programs," "I benefited from service offered," "I had a good experience with the agency," "I know the staff and respect them," "Philanthropy is a tradition in my family," "I was taught as a child to give," "I believe strongly in giving," and "I get satisfaction from giving to a worthwhile cause."

Why Don't People Give?

If people were asked why they do not give to a nonprofit, the fund raising students said these answers were the ones they would generally give: "I don't know how," "I was never taught to give," "Too many organizations are asking," "Too much of the gift will be used for administrative costs," "I don't have the money to give," "If I give to one, I will have to give to all," "The money really does not go to programs," "I was never thanked for previous gifts," "I can't get any information about how the money is used," "I don't know the organization," "I don't understand why people should give," "Children don't need the money," "Don't taxes do the job?" and the famous "I gave at the office."

Why Don't People Like to Ask for Money?

If people were asked why they do not like to ask others for money, the fund raising students thought these would be the kinds of answers they would give: "I'm afraid of rejection," "Asking is begging," "I'm afraid of failure," "I don't know how," "It's an invasion of privacy," "It's imposing on a friend," "It's taking advantage of a friend," "The person I ask may swear at me," "It is demeaning to ask," "Friends will cross the street next time they see me," "I feel a fear of reciprocity (if I ask you, then you are entitled to ask me back)," "I haven't given," and "I will feel uncomfortable asking."

The Fund Raising School has conducted classes in many different countries, in Australia, New Zealand, Canada, Jamaica, Austria, the Czech Republic, Mexico, Tunisia, South Africa, Russia, and more. At each of these sites, whatever the language, the *first response* offered to the question Why don't people like to ask for money? is fear of rejection. (Does this establish that the desire to be accepted and loved is a universal phenomenon?)

What Solicitation Is Really Like

The instinct for giving and sharing is felt by people throughout the world. Its activating forces are love, concern, and the desires to reach out to help, to become part of an exciting program, to share the excitement of accomplishment, and to get on the bandwagon when success becomes certain. And there are many, many other valid reasons.

Thus, solicitation is not as frightful as many people think. Keep in mind that philanthropy is not a practice recently introduced to our society. Over the centuries, individuals have advocated one cause or another and have sought financial gifts from each other to support those causes. We can surmise that they survived the asking. Philanthropy and the gift solicitation process is not as difficult nor as hazardous as people fear. It is certainly less dangerous than it was during the medieval period when, it is said, the bishops had to admonish soliciting zealots to cease the practice of enclosing rocks in their solicitation to make them easier to throw through the open windows and doors of churches and cathedrals. Too many stained glass windows were being destroyed, the bishops claimed.

Solicitation is the simple process of taking a concern that might lie heavily on your heart or a project that gives you joy and sharing either that concern or that joyful experience with a friend, an associate, a neighbor, or a known philanthropist in the community. If the person says, "Yes, it sounds interesting. I should like to contribute!" a flash of joy will course through your system, and you will forget your previous nervous doubts. If the response is negative, your regret will be short-lived. At the very least, you have informed a person about your project interests, and it does happen, at times, that a tentative prospect will approach you to say that he or she has remembered your project and really would like to make a gift. When that happens, the thrill of affirmation is quite rewarding.

Rest assured that you will never be hit, abused, or damaged in any manner during a solicitation. Bill Somerville, president of the Philanthropic Ventures Foundation in Oakland, California, urges us "to get away from giving money away to investing the philanthropic dollar in outstanding people with outstanding ideas. It is a more healthy depiction of what is going on" (personal communication, April 1, 1996). It is this view we at The Fund Raising School take when we urge solicitors to focus on the mission and not on the budget needs of their organizations.

Solicitation possesses a hierarchy of processes, along with certain precepts that must be heeded in planning the approach to the potential donor. These processes are financial peer-to-peer solicitation, other peer-to-peer solicitation, institutional solicitation, and team solicitation. The process that is chosen then sets the pattern for the selection of the team or individual to conduct the solicitation.

Peer to Peer: On Equal Financial Footing

At the top of the solicitation hierarchy, at the peak of the solicitation priorities, is the process of peer asking peer, particularly when a large gift is sought. The peer who will carry out the solicitation generally is the social and financial peer of the potential donor and, thus, should be able and willing to give at an equal level with the prospect.

The implications here are that generally, the social and financial peer will have access to the prospect, will possess a value system that reflects the prospect's, and will feel comfortable asking for the gift. A prerequisite is that the solicitor has made his or her gift prior to the solicitation and at a level consonant with the gift amount that will be suggested to the prospect. If the solicitor's gift has been made, he or she will be prepared to answer with pride and conviction when asked the inevitable question, "What have you given?" If the solicitor has not given at a level commensurate with his or her means, he or she will refrain from asking for a particular amount, hoping that a gift will be offered anyway. But if it is offered, it will be far below the suggested asking amount because the prospect will suspect that the solicitor lacks conviction about the program, has not given, and therefore is not capable of asking for a certain sum.

At this point, the reader may be asking, If my organization does not have people who are the financial and social peers of people at the level where we would like to solicit, does this mean we cannot ask for the large gift? Read on, because under appropriate circumstances, it is still possible to ask for these major gifts.

Peer to Peer: On a Friendly Footing

The second level of the hierarchy of solicitation offers some counsel for action when the institution is not able to recruit volunteers or hire staff able to solicit at the previous level.

Again, if possible, the solicitation should be peer to peer, but the solicitor may not be the financial peer of the prospect but a good friend. And again, the solicitor should have made a gift, one that the prospect would consider quite generous in light of the solicitor's financial status. It will not be necessary for the solicitor to state the gift. This is a case of the proportionate giver, a person whose income and asset holdings may be relatively moderate but who is prone to give generously to various causes. Prior to the solicitation, the solicitor must be on record with a generous gift, one within the solicitor's range but one of which he or she is proud. During the asking process, the quiet message being communicated to the prospect is, "Give in proportion to what I have done." That commitment and confidence will reach out to touch the spirit of the prospect, inducing a gift. The question, "How much did you give?" will not be asked. The prospect will understand that the solicitor does not have the capacity to match the donor's gift but, intuitively, the donor will know that the asker has made a significant gift.

The Organization Asks: Stepping Up to the Challenge

Situations arise when it will be necessary for the institution to ask. Even though it is not possible to arrange a peer-to-peer situation for one reason or another, opportunities should not be lost. A solicitation team, representing the organization, can be enlisted from the ranks of the program and support staff.

The available players in this scenario can be the chief executive officer, the chief development officer, experienced members of the development staff, the chief financial officer if there is one on staff, the program director, and key program staff who are knowledgeable and can speak with conviction about the work of the organization. In each case, it is necessary for these key people to be on record as contributors as an expression of their acceptance of the values inherent in the organization's statement of mission or vision. Any reluctance on their part to give will blur their commitment and mute their voices during a solicitation.

With training and practice, these individuals can fulfill several important roles—as primary solicitors, as expert witnesses, and as backups to support the efforts of a reluctant volunteer. A major inhibition that poses itself as a problem for board members and key volunteers is their belief that they suffer from knowledge deficiency. They think, "I don't know anything about anything. If a prospect should ask me a question, I won't be able to answer it. I can't quote statistics about budgets, programs, staff responsibilities, or the purpose, details, and values of our programs. I really do suffer from severe knowledge deficiency. I'm not able to answer questions because I don't know the answers. I'll embarrass myself and by doing so, I'll embarrass my friend, the prospect. I don't want to solicit, Period!"

In this situation, knowledgeable staff members can serve as *expert witnesses* (discussed further in the next section) shoring up the confidence of the volunteer solicitors.

I have once before described the chief executive officer as the lengthened shadow of the organization. This person reflects the mission and the vision of the institution. Accordingly, he or she is a proper person to solicit a major gift. Another reason the chief executive is an appropriate solicitor is that certain individuals holding significant assets prefer to tender their gifts to the organization's top executive, particularly if the nonprofit is a major mainline institution. With some persuasion, the chief executive can be induced to participate in a solicitation in a variety of roles. By the same token, the development officer and perhaps other members of the development staff should be willing to accept a soliciting assignment. The same goes for the chief financial officer, the program officers, and members of the program staff.

Team Solicitation: Adding Value

All activity comes to an end during campaign plateau time. No solicitations are carried out. This is desperation time for the directors of annual fund or capital campaigns and for campaign committees. It is also the time for the campaign director to activate the buddy system in an effort to cure the crippling infirmity that is calling the campaign to a halt. Many organizations activate the buddy system in times of fund raising stress. It is a simple means of engaging people when fund raising goes inert on the insidious plains of the campaign plateau.

In this buddy system, selected staff members are asked to serve as expert witnesses, teaming up with recalcitrant volunteers who are not carrying out their solicitation assignments. These volunteers' buddies will be able to respond to questions about budgets, fund raising costs, programs, and so forth, and can assure the prospect that contributed funds will be used responsibly. Veritable repositories of knowledge, they will constitute the comfort zone that will put the solicitor, and the prospect, at ease.

The campaign director (development director) typically should accept the responsibility of assigning appropriate staff to team with specific volunteers who have accepted solicitation assignments but who are not reporting results. The assigned staff person will be asked to call the solicitor to suggest several possible visitation dates and to ask the solicitor to set an appointment time for the visit. Once the appointment is made, the team should meet to rehearse the solicitation. Rehearsal is an imperative. When visiting potential donors to ask for major gifts, the soliciting team should be thoroughly prepared. At this rehearsal, all confusions should be dissipated, all questions answered, all knowledge of the prospect and his or her special interests, objections, and extent of involvement with the organization should be shared. There should also be agreement on the protocol to be followed during the solicitation.

The Solicitation Process: A Scenario That Works

The primary piece of advice that can be offered to individuals who have not previously undertaken to ask for a major gift is to relax. This is a normal solicitation, not combat. No one will be hurt during the encounter. A factor to remember is that the process will entail more listening than talking. Experienced practitioners of the art of solicitation maintain that the solicitor's listening-talking ratio is 60:40. As solicitors, we listen the bulk of the time; the rest of the time, we discuss the case, we answer the prospect's questions, and we respond to objections before asking for the gift.

The art of thoughtful listening requires us to turn off our sending apparatus and to turn on our receiving apparatus so that we can absorb everything the prospect is saying. Careful listening to the spoken word should be accompanied by attention to the body language that at times may be more eloquent than words.

The solicitation sequence for major gifts, then, follows the scenario described in the rest of this section.

Step 1: Decide Who Should Ask

Solicitation is ideally made by a financial and social peer who has made his or her own gift at a level somewhat commensurate with the prospect's ability to give, who is compatible with and has access to the prospect, and who is knowledgeable enough to respond to questions about the organization, its mission, and its vision.

The peer solicitor may request a team approach, with the chief executive or director of development joining the solicitor. When the chief executive (or the development officer) and the solicitor form a team, they should rehearse, as described earlier, spending time together to share information and to discuss solicitation strategy and procedures. This important preparation involves some obvious decisions, such as determining who will ask for the gift and agreeing that if the solicitor cannot remember budget figures and program statistics, he or she will turn the discussion to the staff person, who will have the information.

Step 2: Open the Meeting

Every face-to-face solicitation (the most effective solicitation) must start with an opening that sets a proper atmosphere for the discussion that will ensue. The solicitor should begin with the usual opening amenities that pass between friends when they meet and with the introduction of any staff member who is also present.

There will be a logical flow from the opening amenities to the solicitor's explanation of the purpose of the meeting, describing specific needs in the community that must be addressed and the effectiveness of the organization's program. This sets the stage for the discussion that will follow. That discussion should not be drawn out. It must be to the point because, remember, the big question in the prospect's mind is, What do you want?

Step 3: Involve the Prospect

The presenter must be prepared to move from the monologue of the opening section of the solicitation to the dialogue that will characterize the second section and that will seek to evoke responses from the prospect: expressions of interests or statements of objections; declarations of admiration for the organization's accomplishments or complaints about certain perceived deficiencies or neglect—such as, "You never responded to my request for a copy of your financial statement."

Objections, criticisms, and complaints should be answered calmly, in a reasonable tone. Objections should never be challenged, nor should the prospect be chastised as a thoughtless, unreasonable lout. That is, of course, if the solicitor wants to move to the final stage, asking for the gift. The solicitor is there to ask for a gift, not to win an argument.

It is not politic to put your prospect in a rage just before asking for the gift. Do not debate the objections posed by the prospect. Do not belittle the objections. Acknowledge the objections, then endeavor to overcome them by switching to descriptions of positive accomplishments. Listen carefully to questions. Respond as thoughtfully as possible, again turning to a positive feature of your program before moving to closure. Try to establish a common ground for your discussion in order to move to asking for the gift and, it is to be hoped, to move to agreement about the gift.

Step 4: Ask with Confidence

The ask and the close do not have to be a frightful experience. Three reactions pretty much represent the possibilities: "Yes, I will be able to help"; "No, I am not in a position to help"; and "I want to think about this and to discuss it with my spouse [or financial adviser or some third person]."

Therefore, the ask is neither difficult, embarrassing, or threatening. Your prospect has been curious from the beginning, wondering, How much is this going to cost me? or, I wish that he [or she] would get to the point! So, it is important to get to the point. It is not unknown for a prospect annoyed by the procrastination of a nervous, unsure soliciting team to walk out of the room, terminating the discussion. The team must prepare, repeat prepare, the crucial question and practice, repeat practice, asking it, doing it in a manner that will not offend the listener. Try something like the following: "Mr. [or Mrs. or Ms.] Prospect, you have been very thoughtful with your questions and with comments about our program. I have a feeling that we and you are walking the same path of interest and support for this important work. As we have stated, we are in the critical stage of launching our annual fund. Our goal this year is $200,000. This represents an investment in people's lives, in their well-being. You have been involved in other fund raising efforts, I know. You are aware that the smaller gifts are important, but they will not help us to reach our goal. Gifts at the level of $2,500, $5,000, and $10,000 will make a difference in our program and will induce others capable of giving at that level to give. Will you join with us in this major effort? Will you consider an investment of $10,000 in this precious human service? Your gift *will* make a difference. Will you join us in this work? You will have the satisfaction of knowing that you will be touching the lives of many people in this region."

Step 5: Sit Back and Listen

Having said that, having established a possible gift level, sit back and keep quiet. Give the person the time required to consider the asking figure. Do not interrupt. Keep your eyes on the prospect part of the time, but switch to look at the floor and out the window. Turn back to the prospect; watch for body signals that may be communicating a variety of messages to you. If you speak at this point, your tendency will be to utter something negative, something that will confuse your prospect, such as "Mr. Prospect, really, I am surprised that I would have the temerity to suggest such an outrageous figure. I would be ecstatic if you were to offer me $1,000."

This has happened to a nervous volunteer solicitor in my presence. It is most unfortunate because it demeans the process. And it is an affront to the prospect, who is now confused. It is a self-put-down for the solicitor, who has wasted everyone's time, and the chances are quite strong that the solicitor has alienated the prospect, who will give the $1,000 just to terminate an encounter that is becoming embarrassing for all parties.

Give the prospect all the time required by the decision-making process. Stay with the suggested figure. Listen carefully to statements that might sound like a no, such as, "Every time I turn around, someone is asking me for some money." The prospect saying this is deliberating between a yes or no. A possible response to such statements is, "Yes, many not-for-profit organizations are performing valuable human services that signify the deep concern of the people of our country and their willingness to support this work. For example, our program is dedicated to alleviating hunger [or whatever function is appropriate]." That is, emphasize the positive and then ask again: "It would be wonderful if you could join with us in this endeavor by making your gift today. Your $10,000 could make an immediate difference in our work."

Step 6: Respond with Kindness, No Matter What

If the prospect declines to give, express gratitude for the privilege of the visit. If the person demurs, saying, "I'll have to think about this," suggest a date for a follow-up meeting. Offer alternate dates: for example, "Would you prefer a Thursday afternoon or early Friday morning?" If both choices are denied, suggest others.

When the response is yes to a request for a gift, an expression of thanks at this moment is not only appropriate but required. But do not overdo. Some volunteers, and some staff, also, happy to receive the gift, relieved that what they thought would be an ordeal turned out to be a pleasant experience, will chortle on about how grateful they are. They repeat and repeat how grateful they are, how indebted they are to the donor, and how much of a difference the gift will make in their organization. In essence, they try to repeat the presentation. The expression of gratitude should be sincere, and it should be short, *unless* the donor should want to discuss some aspect of the organization's work. Otherwise, say a sincere thank-you and then depart.

Conclusion

Within twenty-four to forty-eight hours, several letters of gratitude should be dispatched to the donor—from the volunteer solicitor, from the chief executive, and from the board chair. In addition, the chief executive officer should call during the week to say thank you. It will be important to develop and maintain a relationship with the donor, a relationship that should make it clear that this person is an honored stakeholder in the organization and therefore entitled to periodic reports about the progress of the programs. Maintaining this relationship is true stewardship.

Finally, remember always that fund raising is the gentle art of teaching the joy of giving. Go forth each day to teach that joy with pride and gladness.

Chapter Five

It's All About Being Friends
Cultivating Donors

"Behavioral Initiatives Imperative to the Identification and Cultivation of Supportive Constituencies and Individualized Interrelationships": that is what I could have called this chapter, using the jargon of the social sciences. But that title, although literally accurate, does not describe the *spirit* of what I want to talk about, which is how you make and keep friends.

My belief that establishing sound relationships with donors is really about being friends was reinforced recently by Sam Henderson, age nine, the son of Eliot "Skip" Henderson, a highly competent, highly respected fund raising consultant in the San Francisco Bay Area. Skip asked Sam to join him for breakfast one morning so that he could interrogate the young man about developing and maintaining relationships. The objective was to encourage Sam to expand his friendship ranks. Sam's creative ideas, displayed in the following list, not only indicate that this young man is having minimal problems engaging friends but also (with appropriate modifications to an adult ethos) should stimulate our thinking about developing and maintaining donors.

This Is How You Make and Keep Friends

1. Invite people to play with you.
2. Talk to your friends.
3. Join the Scouts.
4. Don't call names.
5. Go over to the kids you see, tell them you're new here, and ask to play.

6. Don't be mean to them.
7. Make them laugh.
8. Play with them a lot.
9. Take them places.
10. Help them.
11. Share.
12. Give presents.
13. Stay in touch.
14. Say something nice about their stuff and what they do.
15. Listen to what they say.
16. Focus on stuff that other people do.
17. Say thanks.
18. Don't take stuff away—ask if you can use it.
19. Cheer for each other.
20. Find out what they want.

And also cheer for the wisdom that comes from the creative and active minds of children. It is not a whim to find in the delightful thoughts of a young person ideas to help mature fund raising professionals cope with the complex strategy of building and maintaining relationships with donors. The task of *acquiring* donors is a difficult one. Yet, it is only the beginning. The stability of the donor base is also crucial to the process of fund raising. Thus, donors must be *retained* to ensure financial stability for the organization. Additionally, an expanding donor base gives evidence of a stable, supportive constituency, and accordingly, public acceptance of the organization and its mission and vision. So many times, donors, especially major donors, judge the worth of a nonprofit organization by the depth of its constituency loyalty as well as by the worthiness of its programs.

An unsettling thought for nonprofits is that people do not have to give. If they do give, they do not have to give to your organization. If they do give to your organization, they do not have to make a large gift. They can spend all of that money in the marketplace, purchasing something of interest to them. They can invest it, play with it, or even throw it away. They do not have to give their money away.

Giving is not an obligation, a requirement, or a responsibility. *It is a privilege.* If people give to your organization, they are exercising that privilege, and they are paying tribute to your mission and to the value of your programs that are serving the public good.

Attention to donors' needs is an essential function of any development office, a function that should be taken seriously by every member of the staff. To neglect a donor, to ignore the requests, the comments, the complaints, or even the demands of a donor, is almost sinful. To exercise proper stewardship, and admittedly to satisfy the critical financial needs of the organization, staff should pay careful attention to their donors, large and small. Treat donors gently, respond thoughtfully to their requests, and let them know that they are very important people, because they are.

Read the testimony of Cecil H. Green when this well-known philanthropist and his spouse were honored on the occasion of the dedication of a hospital in their names. The hospital had received a major benefaction from these highly respected donors, and at the dedication, Green explained the philosophy of giving that he and his wife shared:

> The vital point I want to make is the gifts Mrs. Green and I have made . . . are a product of intimate exposure, not *selling*. If there is a any element of selling—then it was a case of our selling ourselves and we became partners in the enterprise. I have thus demonstrated to myself that the larger gifts tend to result from *knowledge, personal interest,* and finally *involvement,* rather than routine solicitation.

> It is this type of involvement which naturally led to the gifts we have made—the reward being the consequent pleasure that the experience has given to us.

The public and the professional press are telling us that competition within the independent sector will increase in the years ahead, owing at least in part to governmental policy changes intended to transfer certain social programs to institutions in the independent sector, to modify income taxes, and to reduce or eliminate capital gains taxes—all of which will affect our ability to secure planned gifts. Even if these policies never materialize, the heightened competition will affect the programmatic structure of the nonprofit organization and will have major impact on fund raising. It would be wise for development officers to write a scenario that dramatizes the possible threats that may affect the development staff's ability to acquire, retain, and upgrade donor gifts. The development officer can then write a crisis plan that addresses what the organization would do if the scenario came to pass.

How alert should an organization's overall staff, development staff, development committee members, chief executive, and governing board be to the fact that fund raising may be challenged by governmental actions affecting nonprofits?

If fund raising is to be challenged, the organization with a crisis plan will be in a position to cope with the many aspects of that challenge. If the threat does not manifest itself, the fund raising function will still be in a strong position for expanding and enhancing its continuing fund raising effort because, in the process of anticipating such threats as, say, the sudden termination of an important government grant, the staff and board will have considered and tested a variety of fund raising contingencies.

What does this have to do with strengthening our abilities to acquire additional donors, to retain these donors, and to upgrade their giving to enable the organization to serve its mission faithfully? A great deal. The focus of the development department should be constantly on the health of the donor base and the contingencies that might affect that base. Additionally, the nonprofit must continually take account of its outreach and its accountability to its stakeholders, its constituency.

The "What If" Scenario

What crises may impose themselves on the institutions of the third sector? There may be changes in the tax laws, either to reduce or totally eliminate tax deductibility for charitable gifts or to reduce taxes on capital gains. Thoughts have been aired about transferring certain human services from government agencies to nonprofits, without commensurate state or federal funding to alleviate these added burdens, which would then have to be countered by more aggressive fund raising. There have also been frequent discussions suggesting additional regulation or licensing for fund raising practitioners.

Planning for such crises as these compels staff and trustees to sensitize themselves to changes within their nonprofit's environment and to anticipate changes waiting in the wings, about to descend upon innocent unsuspecting organizations. A crisis plan should be tantamount to a strategic plan, addressing issues of importance to stakeholders, by whom I mean not only donors but also trustees, staff, clients, donors, funders, volunteers, vendors, and regulatory bodies. To get started on writing the scenarios that crisis plans will address, seek the help of several imaginative people: staff, trustees, or volunteers who enjoy writing fiction or just plain writing. You might give them some sample scenarios to get them started. Exhibit 5.1 contains two of these sample scenarios.

Use your imagination. Select scenarios that bring terror to your total being. It is possible that they will never come to be. But it is also possible that they will come to be. That is why the preparation of a series of crisis plans will not be a waste of time. If the eventualities we envision should impose themselves on our sector, our organizations will be able to cope with them. If they should pass by like puffy clouds on a summer morning, the scenario writers will not have wasted their time. Our organizations will be better prepared to accept and survive whatever challenges may threaten them.

To Weather Crises, Cultivate Donor Interest

What course could nonprofits follow if, for example, both the state and federal governments were to eliminate the tax deductibility of the charitable gift? Is this possible? Nonprofit organizations would be wise to consider that it can happen, hope that it will not, and work sensitively to strengthen their bonds with their constituents, with the hope that these constituents are truly committed to continue the nonprofit's work, tax deduction or no. Certainly, one way to cement our bonds with our donors, and indeed our stakeholders, is to seek their advice and their help. Make them privy to some of these threats that are lurking around us now and invite them to one or more scenario development brainstorming engagements. Following these thought-provoking get-togethers, keep the lines of communication open to let donors know that their thoughts and ideas were appreciated.

Nonprofits in many other nations must raise funds without the powerful support of gift deductibility. Most third-world countries do not support philanthropy with any sort of tax deduction. The gift is totally out of pocket.

Exhibit 5.1. Two Sample "What If" Scenarios.

Scenario 1

When we come to the office Monday morning, we find a letter from one of our major donors to the effect that he will not be able to give the $250,000 gift promised for our annual fund. This will kill an important program serving many people. How can we save this program?

Scenario 2

As of the beginning of April two years from now, tax deductibility of the charitable gift is eliminated. Should we plan to close down because the incentive to make charitable giving will disappear? What should we do?

A representative of a South African human services organization informed a Fund Raising School class that South African community service organizations must raise operating money with the handicap of a 15 percent government tax against each gift that is made. Give $100 to charity, pay a 15 percent fee to the government!

Australia's tax support for charitable gifts is quite small. Yet in Brisbane, a magnificent cathedral was built entirely with philanthropic gifts, despite the limited tax benefits for the large five-figure gifts.

Let not Congress assume, however, that these paragraphs offer any endorsement to the consideration of suspending federal tax support for the philanthropic gift. Let members of the Congress heed the fact that this nation is the most generous nation in the world. A 385-year-old tradition of a working partnership between government and the independent sector, with an awesome array of hard-working voluntary institutions, organizations, and agencies dedicated in service to the people of this country, has served this nation well. The tax code has been a supportive, empowering instrument in this endeavor, encouraging the sharing of gifts in the philanthropic spirit to serve the public good.

What, seriously, does this have to do with *behavioral initiatives imperative* to the *identification* and *cultivation* of *supportive constituencies* and *individualized interrelations?* A great deal, as a matter of fact. Over the years of my professional experience, I have talked with staff people, donors, funders, volunteers, and others, endeavoring to get a sense of their understanding of the purpose and accomplishments of the institutions of the independent sector. The majority of the responses have been positive, accepting of the important roles that nonprofits play in our society. In recent years, however, the responses have taken on a different tone. I have come to believe that the citizens of this country are confused, uncertain, perhaps a bit worried about the state of the sector, what with discussion in Congress about the deductibility of charitable gifts and about the possible need to transfer some social service work to nonprofit organizations. Newspaper headlines such as "Nonprofits Take Another Blow on Postal Rate Hikes," "Background Checks Will Cost Nonprofit Funds and Volunteers," and "Government Shutdowns Causing Havoc with Nonprofit Services and Budgets" are cause for concern. About 1.4 million nonprofits submit annual 990AR forms (financial accountability reports) to the Internal Revenue Service, yet in September 1993, Congressman Jake Pickel of Texas reported to the Congressional Ways and Means Committee that the IRS reads only 1 to 2 percent of these reports. The public has the right to be concerned: too many negative messages are distorting the image of our nonprofit organizations, and cultivation of our constituencies is essential if we are to counteract those messages and respond to those concerns.

Cultivation of people can be defined as seeking friendship (as Sam taught us), enhancing an understanding, developing and improving, for the purpose of advancing education, the well-being, the security, and the good health of the people. This explains pretty much what we want to accomplish in working with our stakeholder, defined by John Bryson (1988, p. 52) as "any person, group, or organization that can place a claim on an organization's attention, resources, or output or is affected by that output." Bryson also emphasizes that nonprofits should pay first-class attention to stakeholders. They ensure nonprofits' futures.

The process of cultivating the donors among the stakeholders, much discussed among fund raising practitioners, may at times be seen as demeaning if cultivation is conceived to be the same as manipulation and an affront to people to the extent that individuals feel uncomfortable discussing it. However, fund raising is a people business. Whether we are approaching governments, foundations, corporations, small businesses, or service clubs, we are approaching *people*. We are talking, interacting, negotiating with *people*. Therefore, we have to take our noses out of the computer; we have to place number crunching aside; we have to lift our senses out of the piles of paper that demand our attentions.

We must expand our abilities to interact with people: to respond to their concerns and to answer questions that are important to them. We must listen, we must digest what we hear, we must store this information in a readily retrievable file, and we must review the information periodically to orient ourselves to what our constituents need and want and deserve.

It is easy to stereotype donor stakeholders through thoughtless characterizations. One person might be thought of as just a "special gift contributor." Another one might be labeled a "memorial giver," another an "annual giver." We are prone to think of our annual donors as "habitual," "impulsive," "renewers," "upgraders," or "suspects for special gifts." These terms are quite impersonal, yes? Such tabloid thinking *might* not be too damaging when we are in internal contemplation at our desks or in quick discussions with our professional cohorts, but we must shelve it when talking, writing to, or interacting with real, everyday people. And the wisest course is to stop thinking in these terms altogether.

About the Telephone

The impersonal syndrome has tendency to manifest itself when we use the telephone, write a hurried thank-you letter, or conduct an interview with a grantmaker.

Consider yourself involved in the following real situations and test your reactions. The first situation is a call to a nonprofit to seek information about how to make a gift.

Receptionist: [*The phone rings four times before it is answered.*] Important National Agency.

     Caller: I am calling Mr. Development Officer.

Receptionist: Who's calling?

     Caller: Does it make a difference who is calling?

Receptionist: I must have your name. Who's calling?

> *Caller:* This is Mr. Caller. I wish to speak to Mr. Develop-
>   ment Officer.
> *Receptionist:* What is the business that you want to discuss with
>   the development officer?

If the caller had been a current major donor seeking information in preparation for making a large gift, how long would he or
she have persisted in efforts to breach this icy telephone barrier?
A nonprofit's telephone communication system should not suggest
links to the CIA. Is such extensive interrogation necessary once the
caller has indicated a desire to talk to the chief fund raiser?

What is significant about this exchange? The telephone should
be used as an instrument to welcome the caller, whoever that person is. At least once a week, the development officer should call
the office from home to listen to the responding voice. Is it warm
and welcoming or is it cold and forbidding? If it is the latter, something has to be done. Do any of the responses posed above make
you feel uneasy. Yes? Then it is time to make sure they are not happening on your telephone or to stop them if they are. The next
caller may be a potential major donor.

Another extraordinary telephone experience prone to leave
callers feeling less than delighted, particularly those with good reason to seek information about the institution's planned giving program, is the following:

> Hello, you have reached the nation's primary communication cen-
> ter. We are extremely happy that you are in contact with us today
> because this offers the opportunity for us to explain all of our pro-
> grams dedicated to proper communication procedures.

> Press button 1 to learn more about our extensive program sched-
> ule and activities being offered today. Press button 2 to learn more
> about our summer program. . . . Press button 10 . . . Press button
> 25 . . . If you should want to talk with a human, offer a prayer and
> then sit down to wait.

This lengthy "menu" is then followed by a medley of canned
music. And perhaps all you wanted to do was call to wish the development officer a happy birthday.

About Letters

Then there is the matter of acknowledgment letters thanking donors for gifts. It gives a donor an empty feeling to receive a brief two-paragraph letter with a strained expression of gratitude for a gift when that gift was upgraded, significantly upgraded. There may not even be any reference in the letter to the increased amount. And it will be emphasized that the computer was not at all impressed by the gift if the letter is not even signed.

Bernie White, a highly competent planned giving coordinator who instills a bit of magic in each gift acknowledgment letter she writes at the Minnesota Masonic Home in Minneapolis, commits herself to make each one a personal message. She explains her reasons for taking time to write a personal letter this way: "We seldom use the standard fill-in-the-blanks of thank-you notes. Many of the memorial gifts we receive are for residents of our Home. It would be cold and indifferent to send reprinted notes to *family*. Also, most of our donors are Minnesota Masons and Eastern Star members. Personal notes to Brothers and Sisters are far more meaningful. These people are the reason for our existence!" (personal communication).

Here is a sample (with the names changed) of one of White's memorial gift acknowledgments:

April 25, 1995
Dear Angela:

Thank you for your gift to Minnesota Masonic Home in memory of Bill Condor, who passed away March 25, 1995.

Your gift will be used to purchase what are known as "restraint reduction devices." Although the words seem cold and clinical—they are to the contrary. They are, in fact, cushions, supports, wedges, etc., which are positioned in ways which give our residents more support, flexibility, comfort, and safety. With these items we are able to customize seating arrangements for those with special needs.

These devices will truly enhance the lives of our residents in a very personal daily manner with the gifts of comfort and safety.

Bill was a resident of our home for a short time. We were told by his son that Bill was a very caring person who liked doing things for others. He even mentioned that his dad once purchased $80 worth of Girl Scout cookies: "Dad just couldn't say no to a good cause."

We sincerely appreciate your gift to our residents. We believe the use of your gift to purchase these devices truly reflects Bill's caring nature.

Sincerely,

[Signed by the CEO]

This is a very warm letter acknowledging a memorial gift. The person who received this letter would have to feel good about having made the gift. The explanation about the gift's use was wise; the personal story about the Girl Scout cookies was a whimsical, thoughtful addition. Do you think that this person will be prone to give again?

About Donor Files

Cultivation is getting in touch with people. It is the fine art of listening and learning about their interests, their concerns, their needs and wants. It is communication at its best because it requires us to stop and practice true listening, to ask intelligent questions, and to heed the answers to those questions.

It also requires us to record these impressions in our private files so that we can review them time and again to reacquaint ourselves with donors' interests and concerns. Maintaining good information files does not constitute an invasion of privacy as long as the files never contain anything that would embarrass the person should he or she inadvertently come across any of the text. A good test is to pretend that the person named in the file is standing behind you, reading your words as you write. Will this person be offended by or annoyed with the data being recorded? If the observer would be disturbed, the wrong information has been gathered, and it should never be recorded anywhere at any time.

Sam Henderson, you will recall, counseled those who would make and keep friends to "invite friends to play with your friends" and "talk to friends of your friends." Immerse people in the purpose, the meaning, the accomplishments of the nonprofit's work. Arrange for them to meet the program people who make good things happen. Give them a sense of belonging, a feeling of being a part of the place, a sense of being important to the continuing advancement of the programs. Invite them to discussion or focus sessions where they will have an opportunity to examine and discuss different theses. Ask their opinion, and do not make it an empty experience. Shortly after the session, send them a brief of the discussion to indicate that their voices were heard. Also send them periodic briefings that update them on program developments, capital expansion, or new concepts. Let them know that they are important.

About Interaction

Here are ideas already tested by other nonprofits for improving interaction with donors.

Immediately upon receipt of a significant gift by mail, call the donor to express gratitude for the gift. This is such a rare phenomenon that the donor, taken unawares, will carry on a ten- or fifteen-minute conversation with you, asking questions and sharing impressions. Many donors will follow up weeks after with another gift. You have made a friend.

Organize a brainstorming brown-bag lunch with your donors or with a covey of professional fund raisers. Brainstorm the subject of workable cultivation devices. Be sure to have a person available to record all the ideas—those that are wise, those that are funny, those that are silly, and those that are crazy. Do not eliminate any suggestion at this stage. When engaging in creative problem solving, it is important to record all ideas whatsoever on a large easel pad with marking pens. There are several reasons for this. One reason is to maintain a moving record of everything that is said. Second, each posting demonstrates the fact that each offering is taken seriously. Third, each suggestion serves as a stimulus, prodding additional ideas from the group.

It is when the group's reserve begins to deteriorate into hilarity and inhibition is set aside that the best ideas are offered. Again, do not dismiss them as crazy. Do not set them aside. Discuss the offerings with the group when the hilarity subsides. Valid ideas will make their bashful appearances as group members settle down to examine what they offered during this creative set-aside-your-inhibitions session. There may be some stupid-crazy-irrelevant ideas that fight their way through the hilarity and turn out to shine with the brilliance of their thought. Encourage people in this exercise because it will call forth some great ideas.

Fund raising is not selling. Yet fund raising practitioners can learn much from the truly professional salespersons who must concern themselves with the important task of maintaining their customers. After all, what is the major preoccupation of competent fund raising executives? It is retaining and upgrading their donors, year after year after year. This is an imperative. Nonprofit executives depend on the annual financial production of the fund raising department. If the necessary goal is to be accomplished year after year, fund raising professionals must give first-class attention to donors—whether individuals, corporations, service clubs, or government agencies and officials.

Michael LeBoeuf, in his fascinating book *How to Win Customers and Keep Them for Life* (1987, p. 181), offers some suggestions applicable to the fund raising process. The following list of ideas for cultivating donors borrows some of his points while also expanding on some of Sam's guidelines.

1. Listen to what donors say.
2. Visit with donors whenever possible to discuss their ideas about the organization's programs.
3. Send donors your quarterly or annual financial statements, enclose information about the scope and effectiveness of your programs and about "what's new."
4. Schedule periodic forums to brief donors on program progress and to ask for their questions and ideas.
5. Telephone donors periodically—although not too frequently—to tell them of new developments that may interest them.
6. When you see something in the newspaper or on television about donors or their children, give them a call or write a pleasant note.
7. Knowing what donors' interests and needs are is important, but it is more important to learn what their *wants* are.

8. Break your back to send a gift acknowledgment within twenty-four to thirty-six hours. If you cannot do this, telephone your major donors as soon as you receive their gifts. Make it a friendly, pleasant call. It makes a good impression on the donor. It is a way to keep your friends.

A further suggestion relates to the donor who suddenly stops giving after several years of thoughtful giving. It is appropriate to call the person to explain that he or she has been giving for a number of years but that no gift has been received during the current year. For example, the development officer might say: "We miss your gift because you have been so supportive for the past five years. Have we offended you in any manner? You are a special friend. What have we done to offend you?" Generally, this approach ends up in a friendly discussion, with the ex-donor explaining that it was an oversight and renewing the relationship with a gift within a week.

Your donors are people, not automatons. Pay special attention to them—or lose them. LeBoeuf (1987) offers some additional valuable advice to professional salespeople that can readily be transferred to fund raising professionals eager to maintain their donors for years into the future: The best five ways to keep donors coming back, he advises, are to *be reliable, be credible, be attractive, be responsive,* and *be empathic. Reliable care* keeps customers—and donors—coming back.

Conclusion

Two themes blended in this chapter, both important in terms of what they represent to the nonprofit organization. The first theme concerned identifying, developing, and maintaining donors, because they are the stalwarts that perpetuate the centuries-long phenomenon of philanthropy in this country. The second theme was the troublesome one of the continuing role of the institutions of the independent sector, which now serve this nation in such a glorious fashion. There are uncertainties about the continuing tax deductibility of charitable gifts, about the expansion of regulatory activities, and about the possibility of nonprofits substituting for government in providing a variety of human services.

In view of the uncertain environment for nonprofits, maintaining relationships with our stakeholders—trustees, staff, clients, donors, funders, volunteers, vendors, and regulatory bodies—is mandatory in my judgment. Our stakeholders are our primary advocates. It is crucial for us to be as open as possible with anyone and everyone who has an interest and a stake in the work of the institutions of the independent sector. We must treat them with the same care we give to friends, because they are our friends.

This is the accountability that we have been describing in the text. *Stakeholders* is another word for constituency. We must continue to study and to apply appropriate methods to inform, educate, and involve, and to bond every stakeholder to the institutions and to the programs of our sector.

Chapter Six

Diversifying Funding Sources

Significant differences separate gifts from individuals and grants from foundations. Can these differences complicate to some degree the resource development process, causing confusion and problems? Yes, they can and they have. The antidote? Broad-based fund raising focusing on diversification, using varied techniques, and directing the appeal to every logical available source, particularly to individual donors.

"A gift is money given by an individual, a family, a small business, or associations such as service clubs 'with all best wishes.' By giving, a person is saying, 'Here is some money, keep up the good work.'" So says Bill Somerville, president of Philanthropic Ventures Foundation in Oakland, California. Conversely, "a grant is awarded on a professional basis. The grantor, foundation, government, corporation, or other organized funders have specific expectations about how the money will be used." Somerville made these remarks during an animated discussion of the differences separating personal gifts from grants and the reasons why less-experienced fund raising professionals should keep the differences in mind.

Annual giving patterns tend to separate dramatically nonprofits' four major sources of funds: individuals, bequests, foundations, and corporations (see Table 6.1). One telling point is the amount of money available to foundations for grant distribution ($9.91 billion in 1994) compared to the amount available for gifts made by individuals to support programs of various nonprofit organizations ($105.09 billion in 1994). With reportedly more than one million nonprofits in this country, the vast majority of them seeking grant

Table 6.1. Total Giving from All Sources, 1994.

Sources of Gifts	$ (in Billions)	% of Total
Individuals	105.09	80.9
Bequests	8.77	6.8
Foundations	9.91	7.6
Corporations	6.11	4.7
Total	128.99	

Source: American Association of Fund-Raising Counsel, 1995, pp. 12–14. Reprinted with permission.

support from foundations, $9.91 billion does not seem to be sufficient to the cause. This is indeed a weighty finding because it tends to make a difference between program development and program performance. It points up the fact that foundations do not have sufficient resources to meet the funding needs of all the nonprofit organizations that request grants year after year, and there are not enough foundations to fund the sector's operational needs. However, there are a great many individuals, corporations, service clubs, and merchants in the community or the region who are willing to provide gift support. Note, too, that when governments, corporations, or foundations terminate a grant, the nonprofit is in trouble; individuals, by contrast, do not cease giving all at once. Many gifts coming from many people assure security for the institution.

Because nonprofit organizations must give priority emphasis to the durability and the futurity of their programs, they must heed the differences that characterize and separate funding sources. A nonprofit's strategic plan should spotlight the necessity to diversify funding methods and funding sources for the funding stability that will undergird the continuing work of the organization. To depend solely on single- or limited-source financing is a fanciful gamble that places a nonprofit on a perilous perch. To depend on governmental funding, foundation funding, or corporate giving without a strong backup of gifts from individuals in a viable expanding donor base is to live the life of a steamboat gambler, bouncing from the heights of ecstasy to the agony of despair. The block grants of years past had a tendency to extend hope and then impose despair, giving sustenance to much-needed human service programs in the late sixties and late seventies and then summarily notifying grantees that the funds were coming to an end. Sometimes a generous, well-meaning philanthropist will suffer from similar setbacks and will be compelled to withdraw precious funds, thus imposing bedlam on a nonprofit board and staff.

Too many executives of federally funded organizations attended sessions of The Fund Raising School in a desperate effort to find a quick fix for their fund raising techniques, hoping they could rapidly replace federal block grants being denied to them after they had received a series of these grants. The block grants had provided a false security, and these organizations had devoted little, if any, energy to building a donor base with gifts from individuals, small businesses, service clubs, and possibly, churches and corporations. It was sad to witness, for example, the depression of hard-working staffers who had dedicated themselves to plan, initiate, and expand an excellent substance control program only to learn that their federal funds would be discontinued. No quick fix could be both quick enough and substantive enough to help inexperienced staff and board members learn even the basic principles of fund raising.

Foundation Grants Compared to Donor Gifts

There is both a difference and a similarity between the approach to an individual and the approach to a foundation with the intent to seek funding. As practitioners, we must research each category of potential givers, with the intent to get to know as much as we can about the prospects, whether they are foundations, corporations, governments, associations, or persons.

When we consider foundations, we ask for their annual reports and their charter statements, which will inform us of their focus. From the giving history, we learn a foundation's grant allocation patterns and its primary interests: education, health, human services, the environment, and so forth. We can inform ourselves about the range of the grants by recording the high and the low amounts of the individual grants allocated during the foundation's funding period. By studying the report, we can also familiarize ourselves with the names of key executives and primary contacts and gain strategic information about a foundation's giving taboos relating to capital fund programs, annual funds, and so forth.

If we are wise, having studied this information, we will endeavor to secure an informational appointment with the foundation chief executive or, perhaps more likely at larger foundations, with one of the key program directors, particularly the one who would be likely to review our application for a grant. Getting to know the personality of the foundation and its staff, learning the thinking and any presuppositions, and testing any requirements for the formulation of the grant request are important. Listening carefully to the language of the person with whom we are meeting, we file all this information first in our memory and later in more permanent form for regular review and study. Parts of it will reflect the person's ideas, value system, and even program likes and dislikes. In essence, we are asking this person to prepare us to ask for a grant according to the funder's terms and in the way that will be most appealing to the person in the position to accept or reject the proposal.

Once we have established a relationship with the funding source, we try to build on that relationship, in essentially the same manner that we show respect for the individual donor if we are sensitive and wise. For example, periodic report follow-ups are an imperative, and we should invite the funder—perhaps a program director—for a site visit to view the results of our work. Maintaining relationships pertains here just as it does when we are being accountable to our individual donors.

Our preparation to solicit a gift from individuals and other funding sources tends to follow the model that I described for foundations, with some obvious variations. The process of soliciting individuals is significantly facilitated in most cases by the fact that the prospect is already a giver and that the person's name and some important, pertinent, but not intrusive information is on file in the donor base. The person's giving history, program interests, and other pertinent facts such as the names of peers and reasons why past gifts were made are preserved in the faithful computer bank. Such data are a major plus for the fund raising research program. We know that the individual who will consider a request for a gift will react to the passion inherent in the organization's mission statement. Each prospective giver will have one or two, or possibly more, reasons why he or she will give. A discussion of the mission and its implications should touch a spark that will produce the gift. This is the emotional appeal.

Foundations, however, are different in this regard. They are much less inclined to be swayed by an emotional appeal. For example, foundation president Somerville says:

> Almost each proposal that I receive describes a problem and, if possible, makes it sound like a crisis. The reasoning seems to be: "The worse it sounds, the more impetus there is to give money to it." The emotional appeal.

> My job as a funder is to "blow away all of the fog" and look carefully as to whether anything worthwhile is going on. I am constantly asking myself, "What are the factors of quality at this agency?" I'm trying to be objective and to see if the agency is doing substantive work. The assumption is fine if an emotional appeal is being used, but not if a foundation is trying to assess a program objectively [personal communication, April 1, 1996].

Foundations require hard answers to hard questions. The individual giver making a routine gift would rarely subject an organization to such close scrutiny, although certainly the donor will want to be assured that the program will be responsive to the nonprofit's mission, goals, and objectives and that the gift, combined with other donor's gifts, will enable the organization's programs to continue along their designated course. And, of course, the person able and willing to make a five-, six-, or seven-figure investment in a nonprofit's mission will ask more penetrating questions and will require convincing evidence that the nonprofit will merit a gift at that level and will use it responsibly, with full accountability to the donor.

Thus, the personal donor generally gives from the heart. The institutional donor gives from the intellect and according to the dictates of the foundation's charter statement. Foundations, under the law, are required to give away a percentage of their earnings from their investments. This fact causes some confusion among fund raisers with little experience in approaching foundations. Naïvely, they believe that the money is there for the taking. Accordingly, they approach foundations with the idea that they are asking for their share. However, for the most part, it is a foundation's charter that establishes its interest parameters. Trustees and foundation staff observe the guidelines set up in the charter and sometimes additional guidelines specified by the governing board.

Personal donors do not have to give money away. Their philanthropy is not subject to an examination by a review team or by a board of trustees. Giving by an individual is subject only to constraints imposed by the financial resources available to him or her and, at times, by the federal income tax code.

Yes, individual donors do, like foundations, have a variety of interests, but because the discretionary money and assets that they hold belong solely to them, they are in a position to make their own judgments about the distribution of philanthropic gifts. In some instances, family members may join in making a final decision, but for the most part, the final judgment is left to the individual. Unlike foundation grants, donor gifts do not have to meet the approval of any board of trustees.

There are, as Somerville has pointed out, some exceptions to the general rule among organizational givers. Some institutional entities can be approached as if they were individuals. Cases in point include unstaffed foundations that have one or two family members in charge and corporations in which the president decides what nonprofits to support. But generally, those seeking funding support would be well advised to understand the difference between soliciting individuals and institutions.

I have one last thought on this subject. Recognition in response to gifts should vary according to the source. For example, it is inappropriate and not recommended to give plaques, certificates, trinkets, and the like to foundations and other institutional donors. A thoughtful letter of thanks with documenting pictures is fine. For an individual donor, a thoughtful letter and a serious invitation to visit the "shop" is appropriate.

Gifts from Corporations

Corporations operate under yet another set of rules, and corporate philanthropy responds to a different paradigm. Where once the corporate office responded to the call of social responsibility, today's corporate giving is directed by a new concept, *cause-related philanthropy* or *strategic philanthropy*. Social responsibility still flies on the corporate banner, but its overtones resonate to the melody of corporate profits.

Rarely does the chief executive officer in most corporations make the decisions about charitable giving. Craig Smith, president of Corporate Citizen, states:

Downsizing has transformed the management of corporate philanthropy in the United States. Forced to explain why business should give away money while laying off workers, contribution managers at hundreds of companies have come up with an approach that ties corporate giving to that strategy. In short, the strategic use of philanthropy has begun to give companies a powerful competitive edge. It seems that the phrase "cause-related philanthropy" is giving way to a new title, "strategic philanthropy."

"Strategic philanthropy" does include the sentiment of enlightened self-interest, a quality of "quid pro quo" or "what are you ready to do for me?" [1994, p. 105].

In the past, as fund raisers, we looked for linkages with members of corporate boards, with key executives, and with employees who had strategic contacts. Today, we must look to the process of involving corporate employees as volunteers, as board members, as donors, and as advocates for the mission that we are serving. We must intensify and expand research that will lead us to the right approach to the right corporate officer and to the right answer to the compelling corporate question, "What's in it for us?"

This phenomenon of strategic philanthropy will continue into the future, although some funders, corporate executives, and United Ways are giving increasing attention to the concept of *civil philanthropy*. The underlying theme in this view is that our neighborhoods are more and more becoming security centers. The qualities historically associated with neighborhoods—strong families, friendliness, and security that depends not on patrolling police but on neighbor-to-neighbor bonds tying the community together—are being lost. Civil philanthropy directs funds toward efforts to change this trend.

Conclusion

Funding agencies such as foundations, corporations, and governments will continue to play a role in the funding process for nonprofits on a specialized basis, that is, in funding for certain specific programs. However, organizations seeking program financial support must be constantly alert to the funders' changing philosophies, pressures posed by limited resources, constraints imposed by foundations' charters, and dictates promulgated by corporate boards in response to changes in the economy.

The best strategy for fund raising staff to follow is to look to all sources and also to build the donor base by cultivating, involving, and soliciting as many individual donors as possible. One foundation, one corporation, one generous philanthropist may suddenly stop giving, causing panic in the ranks. One thousand or two thousand donors generally do not all go away at the same time. Therein lies our security. Think hard and carefully about this principle and treat the donor base kindly. It rarely lets you down.

Chapter Seven

Classic Mistakes and Their Lessons

All in favor of an Annual Mistake Catharsis Day please gather in the southwest corner of the room. There you will find display paper taped to the wall and an assortment of watercolor marking pens. Select an ink color that matches your personality and write your suggestions for activities that will help us celebrate the Annual Mistake Catharsis Day.

If, perchance, you are without a mistake in your entire career, sit quietly, humbly, patiently. Your coronation as winner of the contest will follow immediately after the awarding of the most outrageous liar's medal to the winner of that contest. Chances are that two contest winners will be the same person.

Yes, indeed, mistakes are admirable teachers. As we chide ourselves for our missteps, we are cautioned to avoid repeating them. As we are regaled with tale after tale of mishaps, they take permanent parking places in our psyche. Is it not strange and yet fortunate that mistakes burn their images in our memories to remind us, time after time, "No, I don't want to do that again!" or, "No, it was foolish the first time. It is absolutely unforgivably stupid this time. Shape up, buddy."

Time and time again, I encourage classroom participants to go forth to make their first mistake, to try something that is completely unreasonable, that will make them feel uncomfortable, that may well cause a senior colleague, perhaps their mentor, to say: "Under no circumstances will you do that. You are going to fall flat on your face. Don't do it. If you do, you'll rue the day forever."

That is the best time to try it. If it goes astray, you will rue it, but you will remember the lesson for the rest of your professional career. If it culminates in success, you will celebrate it for the rest of your life, and your colleagues will call you brilliant!

Classic Mistakes: Test with Caution

Here are six classic mistakes and the lessons learned from them.

Mistake 1

During a feasibility study, I unearthed some information about a possible prospect who, purportedly, had a net worth of approximately $5 million. His name was not on the master list of community leaders who were to be interviewed during the study, so I asked the proposed campaign chair, the board chair, the chief executive, and the development officer about him. Why wasn't he on the master list? "Don't waste your time," was the usual response. "He has never in my memory contributed to anything in this community, and he won't now. It will be a mistake to waste your time."

Of course, I called the gentleman, and much to my surprise, he agreed to an interview. We met for forty-five minutes, and during this period, he answered questions thoughtfully, offering a wonderful insight into the worth of the program, to the giving potential of the community, and to the eventual success of the campaign. So I had to tell him that I had heard statements to the effect that he never contributed to any organization or to any fund raising request. "You are so knowledgeable about fund raising, about the community's potential," I said. "Is it really true that you never give?"

He grinned, hesitated a moment, and said, "I believe you are right. I don't give."

"I must ask," I said, "because you seem to be knowledgeable about and supportive of giving. Why don't you give?"

"Simple reason," he responded. "No one has ever asked me to give."

How many times this happens! There was a simple answer. "You ignore me and I will ignore you" was his philosophy.

I then had to ask my final interview question: "If the findings of this study should support a recommendation to proceed with a campaign, would you be willing to meet with me again so that we could talk about the campaign progress and about any possibility of a gift from you?"

"Try me," was his sole response. We did "try him." We set aside any idea of a very large gift for this first ask, and requested a gift of $30,000. He agreed. Out of this experience came my firm belief that fund raisers should *never, never, never deprive the prospect of the privilege of saying no.* Just possibly, if you hesitate to ask because you are anticipating a no, you may be denying the person the joy of making a gift. Never preempt a prospect's response by letting your nervousness or your hesitancy rule the day, much to your disadvantage. The prerogative of saying no is not ours. It is the property of the prospect. Do not trespass.

Lesson learned: always give the prospect the privilege of evaluating the merits or demerits of the program. Some wonderful by-products such as interest or amazement at the scope of the program or gratification may emerge. Be patient; listen carefully to what the prospect is saying; wait for the answer. If it is yes, express your thanks. If the answer is no, express your gratitude for the time made available for you to talk about the program. Ask if you can meet with the person again sometime.

Mistake 2

In 1954, I was in Syracuse, New York, involved in a capital campaign for the Rescue Mission in that city. The campaign chair was a crusty, determined leader who was much admired by business and professional leaders in the city. The campaign, however, was a difficult one because people were loathe to identify with an agency that extended its services to people who were down and out, mostly out-of-control alcoholics. The chair was determined to press the campaign to success, but major gift prospects were scarce. They were scarce owing to a mistake: a careless, thoughtless piece of instruction to a secretary who had never been involved in any fund raising program and who understood little about the social strategies involved in soliciting and receiving gifts. We were devoting sensitive time to the thorny task of involving and nurturing business leaders with a gift potential of $5,000 to $25,000 each. We had a list of some forty names, each precious and important. Another list represented prospects with a giving ability of $25, $50, $100, or perhaps a maximum of $1,000.

We had accumulated about thirty gifts in the $25 to $100 category at the beginning of the campaign, and these gifts had not been acknowledged. In a rush one day, on my way to meet with the campaign chair, I handed the two lists to the secretary, asking her to send thank-you letters to individuals who had given from $25 to $100 to the campaign so far. I gave no further instructions. When I returned from my meeting, I discovered that she had confused the lists. She had sent letters to the list of our major prospects, including with the letters a printed listing of all donors so far, all below $1,000. That printed list included some of our campaign leaders, who had given small amounts—$35, $50, $75—before the solicitation actually started. There was no opportunity to solicit them before they received this mailing. Capable of giving in the range of $5,000 to $25,000, now they had been inadvertently listed in a mailing as low-level contributors.

A furious campaign chair questioned my birth experience, my heritage, and my mentality, and then he settled down to a serious debate about what I called my intellectual capacities. The final debate votes? Chair 52, campaign director 2, both from relatives.

Lesson learned: never be casual when compiling a donors' list. Check and recheck it. Turn it over to a second person to assess the data, then assume responsibility for the final check. Do not depend on verbal instructions. They can be misunderstood. Submit any instructions in writing. When a list is completed, review it with the primary secretary to ensure that all information is correct. Be careful not to list the name of a donor who has specifically requested anonymity.

Mistake 3

The following experience was one I had when college fund raising many years ago. The college president professed to know about a reportedly wealthy person who, in the president's judgment, was able to make at a minimum a $1 million gift and who had a need to make such a gift in order to restore his self-esteem and his reputation. The president claimed to have some information to the effect that the prospect had returned in disrepute to the community several months before, although he refused to confide in me about the so-called blemish on the man's character. "He has to make this gift if he wants to restore his standing in this community," the president said. I suggested that this approach was a hazardous one and said I did not want to be a party to such an accusation. The president promised that the "charge" of a blemished character would not be part of the solicitation because the man would be well aware of the fact that an association with the college through gift giving would clear his name. In fact, the president thought we were doing him a favor by asking. It did not turn out that way.

After our brief exchange of amenities, the discussion with this prospect turned to the college's program and to the fact that a million-dollar gift would provide a much-needed endowment. The benefit to the donor, said the president then, was that "this gift will cleanse your name. You can buy respectability, thereby restoring your image in this community."

The temperature outside was ninety degrees, the atmosphere in the room was thirty below zero, despite the red-hot vituperative explosion from the prospect's mouth that reduced the president's physical frame from its six-foot height to a quivering six inches. Obviously, the answer to our request for a gift was *no!*

Lesson learned: when individuals agree to solicit in tandem, they should also agree to a thorough rehearsal to prepare properly for the solicitation. This is an imperative. Each step in the process should be reviewed. Never, never should one solicitor upstage her or his partner—volunteer or professional staff—with something that was not discussed during the rehearsal, particularly not a hidden bomb that will explode. There should be *no surprises.* Most of the time, there is little chance to recover from such blasts. Therefore, each solicitation should be thoughtfully planned. The role of each person should be discussed and extraneous elements, such as the college president's crude concept of a value exchange, should be deleted. Each member of the team should be relaxed, confident, and able to participate intelligently in the discussion, with no concern that ineptitude will assert its ugly presence. That was the last time that I teamed as a solicitor with that president. He was always a loose cannon. From that point on, I teamed only with volunteer solicitors willing to rehearse the presentation.

Mistake 4

A competent real-estate broker in a relatively small city asked me to accompany him on a solicitation for a $2,500 gift during a capital campaign. The broker had accepted the campaign position of commercial division chair, soliciting merchants, professional offices, and so forth. We had talked about his own gift to the campaign a number of times, and his answer was always, "I will take care of it. Believe me, I will, but not just now."

When we met with the prospect, another real-estate broker in the community, he accepted us warmly and expressed a positive view about the campaign, commending us on our effort to raise the required funds. My soliciting partner, however, showed himself reluctant to ask for the gift, although we had worked out the process and practiced it several times. The prospect was ready, but there was no movement on the part of the volunteer solicitor to ask. As the social and financial peer of the prospect, he was the proper person to ask for the gift. This was no time for the professional to intrude.

The atmosphere was becoming a bit tense. The prospect sensed this, turned to his friend, and asked, "What have you given?" This was a logical question: an innocent information-seeking request in order to judge what the prospect himself should give. My partner could not respond. His head dropped. He was not able to look at his friend, who, sensing that my partner had not made his own gift, said simply, "Let's talk about this at another time," terminating the interview.

Lesson learned: a hand reaching out to receive should be practiced in the giving process. A person who has not made a gift will find it difficult to ask. In retrospect, I should have demanded, prior to the solicitation, that this campaign division chair make his own gift, demonstrate his own commitment to the program, before asking his peer to do so. We had a serious talk back in the campaign office that evening. He agreed that he froze and that he could not look his friend in the eyes while asking for the gift. Several days later, he made his gift, and he successfully solicited an equal amount from his friend.

Mistake 5

In major gift fund raising, always consider every member of the board a prospect. Too many nonprofits neglect this ancient wisdom and, as a result, lose opportunities to secure significant gifts from these logical prospects. Here is a case in point.

A small church-related college in mid America was offered a $500,000 challenge gift from a friend. The offer was made three months into the new year, with the provision that the challenge had to be matched by an equal sum in gift money gathered as the result of an intensive fund raising program. The deadline for the matching program was the end of the calendar year.

The board of trustees accepted the challenge, then passed on the responsibility to the college president, who had little fund raising experience and a staff similarly inexperienced. Months passed with minimal, often-misdirected fund raising. No progress was made in securing any funds. The general mood was that a $500,000 challenge was too severe and beyond the institution's capabilities. Finally the board chairperson, a nun, asked me and another professional consultant to evaluate the program and determine whether there was any possibility that the funds could be raised.

The picture turned out to be bleak. It was complicated by the findings of a quickly organized feasibility study that revealed a severe communication gap between college and town. Additionally, we learned that the trustees had not been asked to contribute. The board comprised five nuns and three laymen: an attorney, a bank president, and a person at first unknown to us.

Our priority action, of course, was to identify the missing trustee, who was out of town. He turned out to be sole owner of a major construction company, net worth $38 million. A member of our consulting team met with him at his vacation home and discussed the problem "back home" with the college. The trustee was fully conversant with the challenge and annoyed that it was not being resolved. An intense discussion followed, culminating in the primary question: "Will you consider matching the challenge in order to save the $500,000 for the college?" His answer was a condition: "Should I agree to match the challenge, and I have not said that I will, then my gift will have to be matched through a fund raising effort."

His questions and his conditions were reported to the other board members. The responses from them were positive, and his final condition, matching his challenge, was referred to us. We then asked him to head the campaign to raise the $500,000 to match his commitment. When he heard the request, he hesitated for a moment and then, with a sly grin, said, "I will do it." He did it with a flourish. Eighty-two years of age, a respected businessperson, a contributor at the half-million level, and in a strong position to call in his chits, he and his specially selected campaign team oversubscribed the $500,000 goal.

The net results that emerged from what had once seemed to be a complete fiasco were $500,000 from the initial challenge grant, matched by a $500,000 gift from the board member, and $750,000 raised during a two-month campaign to match the board member's gift: total $1,750,000.

Lesson learned: take measure of the giving potential of each member of the board of trustees and carefully plan and initiate a sensitive face-to-face solicitation. Provide an opportunity for *each* trustee to give according to her or his ability. Do not solicit by letter, by an impassioned speech by the board chair during a board meeting, or by wishful thinking in silence. What it comes down to is this: somebody has to ask somebody for some money, eyeball to eyeball! If that task is accomplished, particularly by a dedicated leader from the board who has already made her or his gift, others will be induced to follow. Their gifts will reflect their ability to give if the leader sets the pace with a leadership gift. That is the reality of fund raising.

Mistakes to Avoid

The following list sums up mistakes that it is wise to avoid:

- Assuming that board members will give and that face-to- face personal solicitation is not necessary.
- Naïvely assuming that Murphy's Law will never stake a claim in your office.
- Not sending thank-you letters to donors within twenty-four to forty-eight hours.
- Not calling a donor who has returned a $50, $75, or $100 gift in response to a mail appeal, to say thank you.

- Not stopping periodically to evaluate the progress in the matter of acquiring, renewing, and upgrading gifts.
- Not evaluating all aspects of your program at least once a year.
- Not hiring a competent consultant to perform a periodic full program audit.
- Urging donors to give *this* year, before tax laws change and giving is made less advantageous. (What will your story be next year?)
- Submitting to the popular belief that a recession is a bad time to request gifts and not asking.
- Not setting a regular date and time to meet with the chief executive to discuss program progress and review problems.
- Not suggesting solutions to those problems, for review by the executive.
- Not making your own gift, pleading that you are underpaid and that that constitutes your gift.
- Not reading books, periodicals, and occasional papers about various aspects of your profession.
- If you are an executive director, assuming that fund raising is not part of your responsibilities and not making yourself available to your development staff for periodic conferences and the solicitation of special prospects.
- If you are a board member, seriously believing that occasional attendance at board meetings represents your total responsibility, that mission and vision are buzz words, and that giving and asking and attention to the nonprofit's financial condition are someone else's concern (and then boasting to friends and associates that you understand the meaning of stewardship and trusteeship).
- If you are a development officer, entering the profession to earn a good living and not to give of yourself as a servant leader in dedication to the public good.
- Believing in the fable that funds can be raised without a serious examination of all facets of the program planned for annual fund, capital campaign, or endowment and planned-giving fund raising. Shooting from the hip in this activity is foolhardy—and perhaps the worst, most damaging mistake a nonprofit can make.

Conclusion

Learning to do it right is heeding the written and unwritten rules of fund raising. It has been said before many times that fund raising is a relatively simple process. But do not let it fool you. It *is* a demanding taskmaster. Sometimes, it is like a huge jigsaw puzzle and, at other times, like a chess game played by two masters. It requires concentration and an intense focus to avoid the kinds of mistakes that will bring all activity to an end. Listen again to the words of Roger Craver: "You can raise considerably more money with organized fund raising than you can with disorganized fund raising." The time spent on serious analysis, planning and organizing is rarely lost time.

Chapter Eight

Evaluating Fund Raising Programs and Capabilities

Peter F. Drucker writes that we are in a transformative period, a period in which specialized knowledge is the primary resource for the individual and the economy. "Land, labor, and capital," he explains, the economist's traditional factors of production, "will not disappear, but they become secondary. However, specialized knowledge by itself produces nothing. It can be productive only when it is integrated into a task. In a new society of knowledge," Drucker challenges, "managers must be prepared to abandon all knowledge" (1992, p. 42). This is an interesting concept, one that should pose a number of questions for nonprofit board members, chief executives, and particularly members of the development staff.

What is meant by Drucker's phrase, "managers must be prepared to abandon all knowledge"? And what implications does abandonment of knowledge have for managers of fund raising programs? Perhaps most simply, what these questions signify is that, in Yogi Berra's words, "the future ain't what it used to be." Indeed it "ain't." We are living in a perplexing era of change, and we must adjust our thinking—abandon our traditional knowledge, and seek out new knowledge—to cope with the complex demands of a changing environment and the enigmas awaiting us in the future. Thus, periodic evaluation of what we do—challenging the process—is an imperative if we are to keep our work pertinent to the moment and if we are to ensure continuing fund raising results in the maze of confusion engendered by change.

If specialized knowledge can be productive only when it is integrated into a task, what problems does that premise pose for nonprofits that diffuse knowledge by limiting access to creative energy and talent within their organizations, energy and talent that are essential to the successful completion of tasks? What damage can be done to the development function by isolating it from strategic skill centers such as trustees with influence, the executive who sets the vision, the program staff with their rich knowledge, the financial officer with his or her accountability, and primary stakeholders with market awareness? Fund raising is at its most sophisticated when it is able to use the specialized knowledge inherent in a richly accomplished team constituted of disparate talents, seasoning, and viewpoints. Without this composite of knowledge, can significant annual increases be recorded in the face of increasing competition, growing complexities in the marketplace, wavering loyalties on the part of donors, and growing donor resistance to mechanically packaged, impersonal appeals? Fund raising should not be compelled to function, as happens so often, in isolation from the talent richness of the organization. Instead, the development officer should be a transformative leader and, as such, should challenge the process by integrating specialized knowledge into the work of fund raising.

Periodic evaluation of the development program by the development staff will provide many opportunities to integrate specialized knowledge into fund raising tasks by involving knowledgeable persons: staff, trustees, volunteers, and donors.

Challenging the process, the key to abandoning all knowledge, leads to purposeful evaluation. A nonprofit should undertake an annual exercise in testing the mettle of its development program. Evaluation is the studious, sometime tedious, process of asking hard questions and requiring hard answers in response. Foundation president Bill Somerville describes evaluation in terms of a bifurcated experience, evaluating both before the fact and after the fact. Before the fact, the stage is set by defining the program purpose, then structuring the program in the form of goals and objectives. The evaluation after the fact should determine whether or not the program activities were sufficient to produce the desired end result. Were the fund raising plan and its implementation effective in raising the funds specified at the beginning of the year?

Of course, there are questions beyond the relatively pragmatic specification of fund raising goals and objectives that should be addressed. Accountability—the fact that funders want some kind of "proof" that money donated is having a direct impact on the causes that funders intend to aid—must be addressed. Probing questions will inquire about impact, outcome effectiveness, quality service, and the like.

These parameters I have been outlining will be addressed in the remainder of this chapter, which suggests the questions an evaluation should ask about the down-to-earth concerns and accomplishments of the development department in its day-to-day struggle to raise the funds required by the organization to maintain its programs. The fund raising activities discussed here should be subjected to annual scrutiny. They should be evaluated not only on the basis of current year income requirements but also on the implications for years ahead. It might be said that a microscopic view can be taken of the accomplishments of the current year. Then a telescopic view should be taken of the anticipated requirements, three to five years in the future.

Donor Relations

In Chapter One, I devoted some space to the necessity of keeping the donor base up to date and of keeping the individual donor *first* at all times in your development team's attention through proper gift acknowledgment, through periodic reports on your nonprofit's progress, and through various courtesies designed to keep the donor or prospective donor close to and interested in your organization. Here are further specific evaluation questions to be asked.

When was the last time that the development office examined the state of the donor base in terms of percentage of total donor responses to the acquisition letters mailed? What was the unit cost of each new gift produced by mailings during the current year? How does this cost compare with mailings in the previous year? Are mail gifts being received in accordance with the last year's experience? More or less during the first, second, and third week of your mailings?

What was the renewal experience among those who made their first gift during the current year? Did more or less renew than last year? Are the renewals maintaining a dollar level comparable to the gift levels of the last fiscal year? If not, are the levels higher or lower?

Has a per gift cost estimate been made for new acquisitions, for renewals, and for upgrades? How does this compare with last year's cost estimates? If possible, make this comparison for the past three years.

Do you profile your donor base as suggested in Chapter One to ascertain the potential for special gifts and for major gifts? Have any selected donors or members of your development committee, your board, and your executive team been drawn into the process to help you identify possible special and major donors? If so, has the process been helpful to you in the identification of prospective large gift donors? How else do you exert yourself to add to your listing of large gift prospects? Have you registered any success in any of these solicitations?

Major Gifts

As explained in Chapter One, major gifts are defined by the organization, by the market that embraces the organization, and by the development staff. The concurrence of the chief executive, the board, the development committee, and the chief development officer that there are valid prospects in the nonprofit's area will shore up the confidence to expand research efforts. It is rare to identify the prospect of a million-dollar gift or even a $100,000 gift in a middle-income community. If such a prospect should exist, at least one of the individuals named here should be prone to know.

What is needed to evaluate the presence of major gift donors is evidence that large gifts have been made in the past to other organizations, if not to your own; your personal knowledge of potential prospective donors; or success by your organization in the solicitation of major gifts. Of course, the most significant evidence of major gift potential will appear in your organization's database. There may be a hidden treasure in that information base. Is the information in that base searched and evaluated by a development staff member who knows what he or she is looking for? Are members of the development committee familiar enough with the financial structure of the community and its environs to assist with the evaluation of potential gifts hidden in the donor base?

Here is a case in point. An organization's database contained 14,000 names of individual donors. Annual fund production for the year was $250,000. However, the organization required at least $500,000 to meet its program requirements. Can annual fund production be doubled in one year's time? Yes, providing that the organization can identify and successfully solicit major gift prospects in its donor base. A simple increase of appeal mailings or the scheduling of additional fund raising benefits will not do it. The feat was accomplished easily in this case with the willing cooperation of the chief executive, trustees, and willing volunteers. The names of all of the major gift prospects came out of the donor base. The potential of that base had never been exploited before.

Do not go mining in depleted gold mines. Go mining in the donor base, in the minds of each trustee, in the memory bank of the executive officer, in the mental depository of the development committee. Ask questions. Record the answers. Study the database, and probe, probe, probe. Here are some important evaluation questions: Is your database up-to-date? Do you know how to read it? Do you, as the chief development officer, maintain your own private cache of names of the most probable major gift prospects? What use do you make of this informational gem?

Many major colleges and universities have successfully pioneered *gift clubs* for the purpose of attracting large gifts on a continuing basis. Gifts generally range from $1,000 to $100,000 at the most prestigious schools. Other institutions are developing *interest clubs*. Regular donors are interviewed so that the school can learn about their interests in certain programs and their concerns about social, educational, cultural, or health subjects such as research and the like. The development office then sets up an informational file in a computer database for each special donor's and major gift prospect's interests. Future communications with them center around their interests, and solicitations are based on those interests. This technique tends to pull the donor closer and closer to the center of the institution.

In your organization, are efforts being made to ascertain, to store and to use such special interests? Or are all major gift solicitations based solely on the fact that the person has money, the organization needs money, and why should the donor not make a really big gift if the ability exists? The idea of appealing to donor interests has merit and is attracting more and more attention. The approach personalizes the relationship with the donor and strengthens it, giving the donor the feeling that he or she is an integral force for program advancement and is contributing significantly to work relating to the organization's mission.

What work is your organization pursuing to promote the interest circles concept? What energy is being directed to that purpose? Have any conversations been held with the primary donors, those whose gifts truly make a difference in the financial stability of the organization or with those who have the ability to make a difference but whose gifts so far are not at the level of their capability?

Is your computer program capable of receiving, recording, processing, and delivering the data you need about donors when it is necessary? If not, what steps can be taken to reach that point?

Planned-Giving Program

The evidence is quite strong that planned giving will play a major role in the realm of fund raising in the decades ahead. There are many reasons why nonprofits should hone their skills in serving individuals who desire to make a gift as part of their estate planning. Each organization should take inventory of these skills. Is the organization in a position to offer such counsel to individuals? Does the development office promote gifts through wills? In its newsletter sent to constituents, does the organization advertise the facts that bequests will be accepted and honored? Will names of individuals who give bequests be listed in a memory book?

Are occasional mailers sent to current and past givers to inform them why giving through their estates, through trust instruments, through insurance, or through bequests is an excellent way to give? Does the organization have access to a competent estate planner in the event that the development office lacks such skill?

The Capital Campaign

Capital campaigns have been facetiously defined by some of the older fund raising veterans as the "moral equivalent of war." Certainly, there are skirmishes and battles to be won, but this fund raising device is not as evil or as difficult as often portrayed, particularly if proper planning precedes the doing.

The capital campaign is an intensive program to raise a large amount of money to meet the capital needs of the nonprofit organization. Its purpose is described as asset building, because money is raised to improve the organization's asset position for constructing new buildings, remodeling existing buildings, installing new and expensive technology, increasing the endowment, and so forth. Capital campaign goals tend to be large. Timelines range from eighteen months to as long as three to five years, depending on the campaign complexities.

A counterpart to the intensive capital campaign is the integrated development program, which encompasses capital needs, special purpose needs, endowment needs, and a variety of commemorative gift opportunities. Embraced in the calibration of needs and in the overall goal of the integrated program is the annual fund. The overwhelming scope of the integrated program, consuming much time, energy, and leadership concentration, simply leaves no room in the strategy for an independent annual fund effort. The goal for such an all-embracing effort tends to be large: from $100,000 to $1 billion or more. The time frame spreads over three to five years. The focus is primarily on the very large gifts. The pace is slow, deliberate, almost ponderous, to ensure sufficient time to execute a well-planned strategy of prospect research, cultivation, and solicitation. In most cases, thoughtfully selected volunteers and staff accept appropriate assignments for solicitation.

Profound questions have to be asked and properly answered before either the capital campaign or the integrated program is designed and launched.

A strategic plan. Does the organization have a strategic plan reaching forward at least five years? Does that plan respond to issues of concern to the stakeholders? Have the chief executive, department heads, trustees, and key stakeholders, particularly those who could affect the fund outcome, been involved actively in the deliberations, investigation and evaluation, and planning and approval for the strategic plan?

Have all needs included in the overall goal been tightly evaluated and justified, so that the case will pass Seymour's test (quoted in Chapter One) of being "copper bottomed and airtight"?

A strong case. A clear, compelling statement of the mission is testimony to the dominant values that drive the programs, values that justify the effort to attain the goal in order to continue the programs to address the human and societal needs. The case must pose a plausible argument why people should give.

A well-defined constituency. The nonprofit has stakeholders. But these stakeholders are people, organizations, and companies that not only benefit from the output of the organization but also affect the input to the organization. Their level of loyalty and commitment can be an essential factor in the nonprofit's decision to implement or to delay the start of a much-needed capital campaign. By denying their support for any fund raising plan—whether annual fund, capital campaign, or endowment—disgruntled constituents, in essence, will be denying the future of the organization, blocking its efforts to raise the money needed to undergird the work essential to fulfilling its mission.

What is the nonprofit's working relationship with the stakeholders who tend to be positive? Will they bend their efforts selflessly to assist and to promote fund raising by giving and being willing to ask others to give? Will they exercise their influence in the community during the campaign?

Community awareness. What is the status of the organization in the broader community? Is it known? Is it respected? Do community members have friendly relations with staff members and with members of the board? Are people aware of the organization's service to the community? Are they appreciative and complimentary in their statements about the organization? Does the chief executive hold memberships in any community service or social clubs or the local chamber of commerce?

What is the giving history? Has the organization been successful at inducing gift money from the community's people; from its merchants, corporations, and foundations; and from any other gift sources in the area? Was this accomplished in the past through such community-based means as house-to-house solicitation, special public events, or special weeks devoted to community support of the organization? Or was it done largely through internal support, with the cooperation of the trustees and other faithful volunteers? Has there been any success in attracting large gifts from individuals, service clubs, foundations, corporations, and other community-based sources?

Continuing prospect research. Does a prospect research subcommittee exist as part of the board's development committee? If such a committee does not exist, who is responsible for carrying out this research? If board members are not involved in prospect research, are knowledgeable leaders in the community recruited to identify major gift prospects?

An efficient record system. Donors' giving history has no value unless it is securely filed in a manner that makes it immediately available to the development staff. Are giving data orderly and properly filed in the computer database? Have the data been verified (for spelling of names and accuracy of addresses and telephone and fax numbers)? Has attention been directed to the storage of data pertaining to family, business, and professional relationships as well as data reflecting volunteer service and donors' gift history? Are these data reviewed at regular intervals to keep them current?

Good communication. Proper communication is a two-way street: transmission and reception. Does your organization reach out to its constituency through such tools as newsletters and occasional informational letters reporting program progress and, in general, explaining the expenditure of gift money? (Accountability for each dollar is not possible, of course, because of the bookkeeping task.) A simple statement such as the following can be used to involve the donor: "Your gift combined with the many others that have been received makes it possible to offer this service to many people."

Available experienced staff. Major gift, capital campaign, annual fund, and endowment moneys come to organizations through the efforts of a highly skilled, campaign-tested staff and the efforts of experienced, willing volunteers. Are competent, development professionals available to staff your fund raising team? Do they have the experience to plan, to organize, and to manage intensive campaigns? If staff do not possess the skills necessary to prod a campaign to a successful conclusion, are management and the board willing to retain a competent professional campaign firm to assume full responsibility for planning and initiating the campaign and then managing it to success?

Have the trustees approved the project that necessitates the raising of large gifts by the instrument of a capital campaign? Have the trustees approved the intensive major gifts program or the capital campaign? Will trustees commit themselves to play a major role in the intensive effort to raise the funds? Will they contribute according to their ability? Will they ask others to do so? Will they assist in the identification and recruitment of community leaders to assume leadership of the fund raising program?

Potential major gifts. Has the organization been effective in solicitations of major gifts in the past? Have records of these solicitations been stored? Are those records available today? Do you have prospects identified as able to make the requisite big gifts at the minimum level of 5 to 10 percent of the goal? Are these individuals, corporations, or foundations still actively involved with the organization? Are individuals who solicited top gifts from these sources before still actively involved with the organization? Do they have access to other prospects capable of making gifts at this level? Will they use that access to ask these prospects to participate in this campaign?

Leadership. Is leadership available? The most precious quality that can be added to a campaign structure, the quality that can truly make a difference is leadership (see Chapter Three). Is leadership willing to lead, willing to make a gift that will telegraph a message to other team members, and willing to ask with pride and to lead with gladness? Will this quality of leadership be available to put the campaign strategy in motion?

Will leadership within the organization assert itself to support the campaign to the end that other staff members will follow that lead by volunteering in any manner that they can to serve? Human resources are a precious force, inspiring others and adding energy to the campaign workforce. Are these resources available?

A feasibility study. Will a feasibility study be authorized? If it is authorized, will it be conducted by a competent fund raising consulting firm or by a member of the development staff? There are some advantages to using an outside firm. An in-house consultant will find it difficult to maintain an objective mien during interviews with the sample of prospective campaign respondents. He or she may have a tendency to debate negative responses. Additionally, the in-house consultant may have a tendency to guide respondents toward positive responses, biasing the study and sharply reducing the validity of the feasibility report and its value to the campaign planning team.

The Governing Board

The governing board is in a strategic position to affect the work of the development team, on the one hand to help it advance and on the other hand to impede its progress by denying any responsibility for associating with or supporting the team's efforts. Do the members of your board of trustees take a sincere interest in the goals and objectives of the annual fund or capital campaign? Do they, individually or as a board, express a willingness to promote fund raising goals and to assist in goal achievement? Do they create opportunities for development staff members to meet with key community leaders to discuss the fund raising goals for the year and for the years ahead?

Do they willingly give according to their ability? Do they accept assignments to solicit high-dollar prospects? Or do they disdain any or all efforts to involve trustees in fund raising?

Will they involve themselves in any plan to demonstrate responsible stewardship in the community by explaining the impact that the fund raising program has had on the work of the organization in service to its mission? Will they serve as ambassadors for both the organization and the development program?

Chief Executive and Development Staff Relations

The chief executive and the chief development officer constitute the primary executive team. They are the heart and soul of the development program. There should be no tension between these two important executives. There must be unanimity between them on fund raising program matters.

Do the chief executive and the chief development officer schedule regular meetings (at least every two weeks) for just the two of them to discuss various aspects of the fund raising process? Are those meetings scheduled at a time, perhaps at breakfast, when interruptions or conflicts with other meetings or duties can be held to a minimum, permitting the participants sufficient quiet time to discuss important fund raising issues?

Will the chief executive facilitate the chief development officer's attendance at each board meeting, so he or she can listen to the board discussion, respond to trustee questions, if asked, and support the development committee chair in extending a report to the board in formal session?

Will the executive accept the development officer as a full member of the organization's management team, thus acknowledging the fact that this person is a true steward, able to interact effectively with the executive, answer questions, and offer testimony to the stewardship embodied in the organization's values and accountability for the use of capital resources, both human and financial?

The Development Committee

Does the board of trustees have a development committee? Was it set up with the assistance of the chief executive and the chief development officer? Was counsel invited from the chief executive and the chief development officer in the selection of the development committee chair? Was the counsel of the chief executive and the chief development officer secured at the time that the committee members were selected? Is the committee chair a trustee? Do all members of the committee give according to their ability, and do they participate in asking others? Do they suggest major gift prospects?

Does the development committee have the privilege of accepting, modifying, or rejecting the fiscal year fund raising plan? Does the chief development officer serve as a staff person to the development committee, with the authority of the board chair and the chief executive?

The Development Officer

The development officer has the planning, administrative, overview, and outreach responsibilities for the development program. This professional must wear a variety of hats if he or she is to press the development program forward to meet the requirements of a complex future. The woman or man who will head this crucial function in the years ahead must be as agile as an Olympic athlete and as pliable as a ballet star, able to move quickly from one stance to another without straining a limb. This person has to be a fund raiser first and then a negotiator, a salesperson, a teacher, a trainer, a planner, a financial expert, a dreamer, a pragmatist, a public relations expert, a market expert, a persuader, a psychologist, and a therapist—with all the virtues attributed to Boy Scouts.

Conclusion

Many demands will be placed on the agendas of nonprofit organizations in the decades ahead. Nonprofit burdens will not become lighter. They will confront greater expectations from stakeholders, governments, regulatory bodies, critics of the independent sector, and donors, who will be approached by many organizations seeking gift support.

Many changes await the development staff, the chief executive, and particularly the governing board in keeping sufficient financial and capable human capital available, defining a mission that addresses a valid community need, and arranging for programs planned, organized, and activated by competent, dedicated staff. To meet these changes, challenge the validity and application of your knowledge base and its pertinence to the job that has to be done.

Part Two

Fund Raising
in Perspective

Chapter Nine

Our Heritage
Rich in Values and Virtues

Fund raising, gift giving, and receiving is so much a part of our national experience that we in the United States tend to accept the practice as home grown, a totally American phenomenon. In its modern day form, it may well be. However, our basic principles of fund raising and philanthropy are derived from the lessons of past centuries, from the practices observed in the ancient Greek and Roman cultures, from the practices found among the Puritan settlers during this nation's colonial period, and from the practices of other cultures in between these. We owe a debt of gratitude for the richness of our philanthropic heritage and the lessons bequeathed to us. So much of what we know and what we practice in fund raising has been passed forward to us by men and women who raised money in this and other lands during the previous centuries. In this century, we have collated and tested those lessons further and added to our wisdom, making fund raising a professional discipline. The wisdom we vaunt today was the common sense of those who preceded us. Some of that wisdom is in this book, and this chapter looks specifically at the early forms of that wisdom.

The very word *philanthropy,* meaning "love of mankind," was deeded to us by the early Grecian culture. Philanthropic practice was recorded in medieval Europe, in Babylon, and in ancient Egypt. In my office at home, for example, I have a framed replica of a letter sent out by the philosopher Moses Maimonides from Egypt to the surrounding communities in A.D. 1170, asking community leaders to help raise funds to redeem captives.

Fund raising in Europe during the medieval period was confined primarily to activities described by Redmond Mullin in his book *The Wealth of Christians* (1984) as charity bazaars and sales. Fairs were staged to support hospitals and leper houses, and fund-seeking letters were used to ask for money to rebuild churches (p. 157). Money was also raised from collecting boxes, sales of relics, and sponsored bell ringing. Official fund raisers were used by some churches to appeal to congregations for gifts to support the church and to build and maintain hospitals and schools (p. 163). During the medieval period in England, a license to beg was required of these official fund raisers (p. 158). Thus, among those carrying such licenses were priests, members of religious orders, and canons appointed by bishops to visit churches during services to appeal to the congregation for gifts for hospitals, churches, and other good works in pre-Reformation Europe.

Our Early U.S. Heritage

Students of fund raising and philanthropy would be wise to read Robert H. Bremner's *American Philanthropy* (1988), an engrossing history of fund raising's journey through the colonial era in this country to the final decades of the twentieth century, the lessons that were learned, and the wisdom that flowed from this learning and was bequeathed to us.

Bremner identifies among the early American philanthropists "those gentle Indians of the Bahama Islands who greeted Columbus at his first landfall in the New World." Columbus reported that the Indians "gave away anything that was asked of them and bestowed each gift with as much love as if their hearts went with it" (1988, p. 7). Among those who helped to found U.S. philanthropy were the Puritans, who sailed the Atlantic "to establish communities on the new continent that were *better* than the ones that they had known back home" (p. 7).

John Winthrop, governor-elect of Massachusetts, preaching to his fellow Puritans as they crossed the Atlantic to the U.S. Colonies in 1630, defined the word *charity* as "a synonym for love," not as aid to the poor (the word's usual modern sense), and the model he proposed was not a scheme of benevolence but a code of conduct for a company of Christians who had entered into a covenant with God: "In this duty of love we must love brotherly without dis-simulation, we must love one another with a pure heart fervently, we must bear one another's burdens, we must not look only on our own things but also on the things of our brethren" (Bremner, 1988, p. 7).

Such beliefs set the tone for the Puritan communities, the spirit for coping with the challenges, the demands, and the adventures of an unknown country. Love would be the guiding spirit for each person, for each act in the wilderness of a new environment. "We must be knit together to this work as one man. We must delight in each other, work as one man," Winthrop said. "We must delight in each other, make others' conditions our own, rejoice together, mourn together, labor and suffer together. The common objective—to improve our lives to do more service to our Lord—must never be lost sight of and 'the care of the public' must take precedence over all private interests" (Bremner, 1988, p. 8).

Winthrop's love was spiritually motivated and as such imparted a particular meaning and a dignity to the word *charity*. It did not have the taint of "doing good" that has sometimes tended to diminish it to a pejorative. Winthrop spoke to the deeper meaning of companionship and concern and respect for each other and to a love of human beneficence as the golden rule that would blend people into a community of souls.

Philanthropy meant "love of mankind" to the early Greeks. The practice of philanthropy among the Puritans was also linked to an idea of "brotherly love." That heritage is still ours. Today, the definition of philanthropy focuses on how that love is to be manifested. Modern philanthropy is "voluntary action for the *public good* through voluntary giving, service and association," according to Robert Payton (1988, p. 32), professor of philanthropic studies at Indiana University.

Arthur C. Frantzreb, a well-known fund raising consultant, in effect relates the philosophy of modern fund raising to the ideas in Winthrop's definition of charity when he writes:

> Funding is the activation force that makes possible fulfillment of human caring about our neighbors, our fellow human beings. Fund raising is not the reason for humanitarian results. The human spirit of caring normally begins with our love for fellow

persons and our desire to help assure normal lives and experience—our human values.

Once we seek to guarantee moral, ethical and spiritual values then the methodology of enhancing values requires fiscal sharing to assure, even to insure, realizing and stabilizing those values. Fund raising, voluntary philanthropy expressing love for humankind, begins with the desire to express human values, assure them, then to insure them [personal communication, 1995].

Age of the Honorable Beggars

Philanthropy in the Colonies existed in a basic neighbor-to-neighbor form. Not much in the way of money was exchanged. Philanthropy took the form of sharing services and joining together to build shelters and to clear land for primitive farming. People's concern for people was the ruling word. If any fund raising took place, it was through the medium of the church.

As the founding of a new nation progressed and the need for nonprofit building and program support funds increased, the hired solicitor entered the fold, wandering the land to seek gifts to build colleges, schools, and hospitals. James Howell Smith's "Honorable Beggars" (1968), a fascinating tale of the evolution of philanthropy and fund raising during the colonial period and later, describes these peripatetic agents of philanthropy, who were paid a fee to travel from village to village and province to province to solicit funds for churches, schools, universities, and hospitals—for any cause that required financial support.

They served well. Among them was a veritable giant, Benjamin Franklin. His primary contributions to present-day strategy were the challenge grant (or matching gift); the pledge, permitting payment of a gift over a period of months or even years; the sequential solicitation; and the technique of thoughtful strategy planning for each solicitation. When the Reverend Gilbert Tennent sought Franklin's help to build a Presbyterian church in Philadelphia, Franklin declined direct help but offered wise counsel that has earned a precious place in the archives of fund raising: "In the first place, I advise you to apply to all of those whom you know will give something, next to those whom you are uncertain whether they will give anything or not and show them the list of those who have given, and lastly, do not neglect those whom you are sure will give nothing, for in some of them you will be mistaken" (Cutlip, 1965, p. 6). Tennent took his advice, Franklin reported, for he asked everyone, and he obtained a much larger sum than he had expected.

The strategy Franklin devised is still in practice, particularly in the solicitation of major gifts. Today, however, it is called sequential solicitation, and it pertains more to strategy of soliciting *pacesetting*, or *leadership*, gifts to set the pace for all subsequent gifts. By soliciting the largest gift first, fund raisers encourage subsequent givers to lift their sights to the gift levels required for a successful campaign.

Franklin admitted to a "bit of cunning" in his plan to raise funds to establish the Pennsylvania Hospital in Philadelphia in 1751, the first free admission and free discharge hospital in the colonies. Franklin was aware that the initial efforts to fund the project were not succeeding, and he realized that a new strategy was needed: if funds were to be raised, it would be necessary to seek a grant from the provincial legislature. He also knew that members of the legislature were not supporters of the plan. Cunning would be needed to induce them to approve the grant. They would not allocate the required £4,000, so he asked for an allocation of £2,000 with the provision that the hospital managers would raise a similar amount from their own sources. Of course, the legislators believed that the managers would fail in their efforts. They approved the request with the feeling that the project would fail and that they would be seen as generous legislators without the expense. Franklin then accepted the challenge to raise the matching funds. He and his associates approached their prospects on a carefully devised sequential strategy, asked donors to give with the promise that the gift would be matched, and offered donors the opportunity to spread their payments over a period of time. Franklin and his associates raised the additional £2,000, and the legislature paid the required grant (Smith, 1968, p. 17). The hospital is still operating today in Philadelphia.

The eighteenth century was the time of pioneering fund raising; the nineteenth century marked a significant period of progress in the definition of fund raising as a discipline. This was the era of the middlemen: the entrepreneurs and the skilled financial advisers who represented the organization and its needs before potential donors.

Scott Cutlip (1965, p. 26) attributes to the "genius" of two YMCA officials, Lyman L. Pierce and Charles Sumner Ward, at least part of the introduction of "systems and efficiency" to the fund raising process in the 1890s. As general secretary of the Grand Rapids, Michigan, YMCA, Ward was frustrated by the constant necessity to give priority to fund raising in order to fund the YMCA's operating programs. He felt fund raising was a burden (as do many nonprofit executives today). He reduced that burden, and the frustration, by use of a simple device. At the beginning of the year, he marshalled the energies of his volunteers: trustees and other supporters. He asked these volunteers to dedicate a small portion of their time each day to soliciting potential contributors for gifts. He promised them that when the task was done, he would not burden them with fund raising chores again until the beginning of the next fiscal year.

Ward's secret? "You can get busy men to give a lot of time for a limited period" (Cutlip, 1965, p. 93).

Pierce, a YMCA secretary in Omaha, Nebraska, also brought new discipline to fund raising. He enlisted a veritable army of volunteers to assist in the solicitation of gifts, and he used a chain of command adopted from the military as a control instrument, both for enlistment and for monitoring the solicitation process. The "army" was organized by squads, with each squad headed by a volunteer leader. These key leaders accepted the responsibility to assign solicitation tasks and to overview the solicitations to ensure that each would be carried out.

Pierce was able to maintain command of his forces and his campaign in good order. Discipline, order, and control asserted themselves. Discipline joined with entrepreneurism to bring stature to fund raising.

The military concept of order obviously had to attract military nomenclature as well. It became inevitable that the volunteer who would head the campaign would be called the general chairman. And it was equally inevitable that the voluntary army would be divided into divisions, battalions, and squads. Thus, fund raising spread some martial splendor among other volunteers, who were given names such as colonel, major, captain, and lieutenant. Fortunately, the working ranks were made up of good, everyday working volunteers.

Others who belong in the pantheon of fund raising are, of course, Dwight L. Moody, the evangelist who offered the gentle thought, "Blessed are the money raisers for in heaven they shall stand next to the martyrs" (Cutlip, 1965, p. 144), and Frederick T. Gates, the young Baptist clergyman and fund raiser who exemplified grace in action in his patient, sensitive yearlong solicitation of John D. Rockefeller for a $1 million gift to establish the University of Chicago as a major institution of higher education serving the virgin West.

Many women, too, have made their mark in the history of philanthropy as fund raising professionals and as philanthropists. Mary Mason Lyon, a schoolteacher with dreams of launching a college for women, in 1830 assumed the responsibility of raising the $30,000 required for the founding of Mount Holyoke Seminary (now Mount Holyoke College). She walked hundreds of miles in her inspired search for funds, which ranged from gifts of six cents up to, fortunately, the necessary larger gifts. Obviously, she accomplished her mission; the school opened in 1837.

Jane Addams founded Hull-House in Chicago in 1889, the best-known of the early settlement houses. Clara Barton served as a nurse during the Civil War, soliciting and delivering the medical supplies that had been in short supply for wounded soldiers. In 1881, she realized a dream. She incorporated the American Association of the Red Cross (which became the American Red Cross in 1893).

I would be remiss in fulfilling my responsibility to reflect our heritage in its fullness if I did not accord credit to the many who contributed significantly to the emergence of philanthropy in our land but who have never been honored. They were many, of many races and many nationalities, expressing a citizenship of the human spirit by their giving of their energy, their talent, or their treasures. They are rarely noted and more rarely commemorated for their quiet gift to the generations that were to follow them. James A. Joseph, author of *Remaking America* (1995, p. 27), has recorded the gifts, the traditions, and the expressions from the spirit of Native Americans, African Americans, Asian Americans, and members of the Latino cultures including Mexicans, Puerto Ricans, Central Americans, and Cuban Americans. Exploring "the impact of Native American traditions on the stream of ideas that shaped the early American vision of community," Joseph explains why political philosophers as different as Thomas Paine and Karl Marx saw the Native American tribe as a model of social organization, benevolence, and communal life.

He chronicles the expansion of the meaning of community and philanthropy that came about through the actions of such giants as the legendary Suquamish chief Seattle, who devoted most of his life to promoting peace in the community; Reuben Snake, a former chairman of the Winnebago tribe of Nebraska and also president of the National Congress of American Indians and a life member of the Native American Church; and Zikala-Sa, a pan-Indian activist, a woman working "on the razor's edge between tradition and change" (Joseph, 1995, p. 59). Zikala-Sa was an accomplished violinist, a thoughtful writer, and a determined activist whose primary concern was to be a servant to Native American people, a voice for the voiceless people. She embraced the Anglo as well as the Native American members of the community. She expressed her vision of a community and of giving back to one's community eloquently, saying, "Life is not worth living if it does not demand some little effort on our parts to contrive in it. It is not what we give for nothing, but what we inspire others to try or to do—that is the best, most valuable gift we can offer" (p. 70).

Two additional philanthropists who must be mentioned are Madame C. J. Walker and Oseola McCarty. Walker, a successful African American entrepreneur and a busy activist sensitive to the needs of African American people, earned a fortune developing and wisely marketing cosmetics designed especially for African American women. She distributed her extensive wealth generously to many causes, primarily the needs of African American women, and she employed twenty thousand women in her enterprises. She served them and others well.

In 1995, Oseola McCarty, an eighty-seven-year-old African American woman who left school after the sixth grade and who earned a living for seventy-five years by taking in laundry, pledged $150,000 to Southern Mississippi University to endow the Oseola McCarty Scholarship for African American students.

It is important to recall that the philosophy of fund raising held by the early giants in the field was based on love, selfless service, a firm belief in the cause that they were serving, and a religious commitment. This philosophy is part of our fund raising heritage. It has imbued our work with its convictions, its conventions, and its stature. For this reason, no one should ever apologize for participating in any fund raising.

This philosophy based on love and selfless service blends easily with the important strategic counsel so often offered by the founding pioneers. It is, for example, reflective of the conviction of Robert Greenleaf (1991) about servant leadership, now so much a part of the general fund raising culture. I have been told that Eddie Cantor, entertainer of generations past, once said, "Service is the rent we pay for the space we take up on earth."

A Test of Fund Raising Concepts

Many philanthropic concepts engendered during the nineteenth and early twentieth centuries were put to the test during World War I when the team of Pierce and Ward, supplemented by Ward's associate Harvey Hill, planned, organized, and implemented a strategy to raise funds for war relief. At the behest of President Woodrow Wilson, seven of the largest national nonprofit organizations agreed to respond to the call for help: the YMCA, YWCA, National Catholic War Council, War Camp Community Service, American Library Association, Salvation Army, and the Jewish Welfare Board. These organizations merged their services into the United War Fund Campaign.

The plan was typical of Ward and Pierce's philosophy of fund raising. It featured a tight timetable to ensure efficient, effective action and a chain of command to facilitate enlistment, assignment, and activation of volunteers throughout communities across the country. All activity was under the control of top volunteer leadership nationally and in the communities. John R. Mott, who was involved with both the Red Cross and the YMCA, was the director; Ward and Pierce served as his counsel. After only several months of activity, the campaign council announced on November 25, 1918, that more than $200 million had been raised. Smith (1968, p. 234) notes that up to that time, this was the largest sum ever raised in such a short period through a voluntary effort. Ward and Pierce's strategy of "systems and efficiency" was authenticated. Their names and their fame were etched in fund raising history by the war relief fund of 1918.

New names and new forms began to emerge in the world of fund raising following the end of World War I. Lessons learned were put to productive use. Talents discovered were marshalled and integrated into partnerships and consulting companies. Out of this activity came professional companies to provide consulting services or full-time campaign direction services to organizations that needed to raise large sums of money.

Here is a summary of the lessons learned in the years before World War I:

Evaluate the market potential.

Base plan on the findings of the evaluation.

Involve and train volunteers for solicitation purposes, particularly members of the governing board.

Construct tight timetables.

Use sequential solicitation: secure the top gift first in order to set the pace for all other gifts.

Use the pledge as a technique to induce larger gifts.

Use the challenge, or matching, gift to encourage others to give and possibly to increase their gifts.

Professional Fund Raising Companies

The records are not clear on the matter of which professional fund raising firm was first to offer its services, although Cutlip (1965, p. 158) credits Ward and his aggressive associate with the honor. Ward and Hill Associates, according to Cutlip (p. 41), was founded May 1, 1919. It was not too long before Ward invited Pierce to join the group and then F. Herbert Wells. Wells's son, Louis, later founded his own firm, The Wells Organization, which specialized in church fund raising. (I had the privilege of competing with The Wells Organization in church fund raising in the 1950s, in Onondaga County, New York. I learned many lessons as a result of this competitive encounter, and the memories are pleasant.)

Christian H. Dreshman, another YMCA official, joined the Ward staff to direct capital campaigns. This set the stage for the founding of Ward, Dreshman, and Rheinhardt, a national fund raising consulting company still in existence. The John Price-Jones firm was founded in 1920 in New York City. I had the privilege of being a staff member and corporate executive of George A. Brakeley, Inc., from 1959 to 1972 in San Francisco. Brakeley's father had been an early member of the John Price-Jones team. I had the opportunity to work with and learn from the younger Brakeley, an elite member of the fund raising community. He is still a friend today.

These and other pioneering companies as well as independent consultants served as seed beds for that remarkable talent that was an emerging professional class. Harold Seymour, whom I have already mentioned, wrote the important book *Designs for Fund-Raising*. Others of the pioneer era wrote the encyclopedia of fund raising in their minds, but that accrued wisdom has never been fully disseminated, much less published. Fortunately, at least some of it is being passed along by those who knew the "old walruses" of this trailblazing generation.

With the founding of consulting companies and eventually professional societies, fund raising was no longer an instrument relegated to entrepreneurs or middlemen. It was well embarked on the journey of becoming a discipline, a profession. Continuing efforts toward acquiring dignity and toward promulgating the ethics of the art among the members of this profession have made fund raising more acceptable to the community at large for the most part.

The American Association of Fund-Raising Counsel (AAFRC) was founded in 1935, made up of the pioneer companies. One of its early acts was to write a statement of standards and ethical practices to guide association members (and all other fund raising practitioners) in the evaluation, planning, and execution of fund raising programs. One of the important standards agreed to at the beginning of the AAFRC's life is that member firms will not base their fees on any percentage or other contingency arrangements. That is, fees are not to be related to the amount of money that has to be raised. They are to be computed by the amount of time and the level of professional services required. Codes of ethics approved and accepted by the AAFRC and other present-day professional societies include a similar statement disclaiming percentage compensation or any other contingency method of compensation for professional services.

Conclusion

Winthrop preached to his shipboard congregation that "'the care of the public' must take precedence over all private interests." Although the modern definition of philanthropy as volunteer action for the public good was not in use during the early centuries of this nation, the philosophy behind that definition has been strongly embedded in the spirit of many heralded and unheralded philanthropists, whose deeds serving the public good entitle them to enshrinement in a pantheon of philanthropy to honor their commitment to the community and to society and to acknowledge their generous gifts, given willingly in dedication to the advancement of the community.

Philanthropy is a legacy we have inherited. Part of our stewardship is to pass it on to future generations. Remember always that the fabric we hold in our hands is fragile. Our stewardship is to protect and preserve it.

Chapter Ten

A Blend of Art and Science

The Five Essential Steps in Disciplined Fund Raising

Is fund raising a science? Or is it more art than science? Fund raisers occasionally debate this issue with no resolution. In this chapter, a one-sided bull session, I offer my thoughts on this subject.

The Random House College Dictionary defines *science* as "a branch of knowledge and study dealing with facts or truths systematically arranged and showing the operation of general laws." Additionally, science is "any skill that reflects a precise application of facts or principles." *Art* is defined as "the quality, production, expression or realm of what is beautiful, or of more than ordinary significance." It is also a "field, genre or category of this realm, skill in conducting any human activity."

When practitioners of fund raising debate whether fund raising is science or art, there are some points they concede.

Facts and Truths

Clearly, certain aspects of fund raising have a touch of science because they require skills that reflect "a precise application of facts and principles." For example, preparations for a major capital campaign require a feasibility study, that is, a thorough in-depth examination of the community's ability and willingness to provide the requisite leadership and contribute the funds to meet the goal. Interviews must be conducted with opinion makers, those with the ability to offer pacesetting gifts, and potential volunteer leaders capable of chairing phases of the campaign. Gift range charts for capital campaigns and annual fund programs must be calculated to predict the quality and number of gifts required to ensure fund raising success. Such charts require computations based on hard facts: How many gifts at which levels will be needed? How many prospects (potential donors) have to be identified at each level to support the required gift production? Science will tell us that not all prospects will give; many will not give at all and some will not give at the level requested by a solicitor. This is a harsh reality that must be respected.

Other items produced from facts or truths systematically arranged and operating according to general laws are fund raising budgets, which require critical analysis and computation, and post-program evaluations and cost-effectiveness studies, which are part of the overall program evaluation process. Direct mail testing checks the validity of the mailing list, the appearance of the envelope, the appeal of the letter's opening lines, the expression of the case, and the actual request for a gift. If all of these information items are truths, and they must be if we are to rely on them, then we are venturing in the direction of a science, are we not?

Imponderables

Yet there are too many imponderables, generalities, and outright reversals in the practice of fund raising for us to pretend that it is always a precise application of facts and principles. Yes, experienced fund raisers bank to some degree on proven formulas. More often, however, they turn to intuition, or to the intelligence bank that some call scar tissue, a compilation in their minds of past experiences—both the successes and the abject failures.

Each experience teaches a lesson never to be forgotten. The veteran tends to turn to this experience bank when counsel is needed. Rather than turn entirely to facts and figures, she or he would rather draw wisdom from that wonderful human reservoir called common sense and its working corollary, dour memories from the past. The wisdom of the elders, seasoned by the humility of scar tissue and tempered by common sense, is our patient guide every day.

More Art Than Science

We may admit that fund raising does, at times, borrow from the sciences, but we most often act as though fund raising is art.

Picture the development officer, for example, directing the definition of the case, specifying the needs, drafting a gift range chart, coaxing a reluctant chief executive and more reluctant trustees to get involved, designing the campaign timetable, planning solicitation strategies, putting all the varied pieces into place for the solicitation of a $1 million leadership gift, pressing for the completion of grant applications to selected corporations and foundations, and training a cadre of volunteers in the process of a major gift solicitation. She or he is like nothing so much as the conductor of a symphony orchestra, who blends the performances of ninety or so skilled musicians playing a variety of instruments into a concert that will please an audience.

The conductor is an artist, and the chief development officer, directing and blending complex concepts into a harmony of accomplishments, is also an artist, working with a blend of intuition and fact, acquired wisdom and hard data. The blend of art and science in successful fund raising, the achievement of a level of harmony, discipline, rhythm, and pleasant acquiescence similar to that a conductor achieves, ought to earn a fanfare of triumphal trumpets and percussion instruments for the development director every day of the campaign.

Truly, it would be wonderful if the aggravating problems that so often complicate an already difficult campaign could be solved with the wave of a baton. It does take a good measure of experience and common sense and a bit of quiet meditation as well as a touch of science to work one's way through the dilemmas that arise in fund raising. Yet the experience, common sense, and meditation are more readily available, and more soothing to the soul, than a complicated formulation.

A Case Study

For example, a dilemma that I faced some years ago, at the beginning of a complicated hospital campaign, prodded me to employ an art form: a process of listening, watching reactions to proposals, asking questions, and probing the desire of the potential contributors to support an effort to construct a much-needed community hospital. This is the art form of studying and planning before taking action. The science that is also present is inherent in the strategic process, the data analysis and critical thinking one does before coming to a decision.

I was the campaign director assigned to the client. The campaign supervisor from the fund raising company for which I worked instructed me to focus my energies during the early months entirely on the solicitation of just one corporation for a gift for $175,000. "Plan no solicitation until after that gift is received" was the edict. "Let that gift serve to raise giving sights of the remaining prospects."

It was a classic case of sequential solicitation, right from the teachings of Benjamin Franklin. Direct your energies to secure the pacesetting gift, then use the force of this gift to set an example to other donors. At times, however, the wisdom of the sages has to be tempered by the reality of the moment. Discrete probing, data analysis, and critical thinking established the fact that the corporation was planning to give considerably less than the suggested figure of $175,000. A failure to get this pacesetting gift would have had a negative impact on the campaign.

During the fact-gathering preliminaries, the campaign chair and I also learned, however, that the employees' gift club at this corporation was considering a contribution of $15,000 to the hospital campaign. Accordingly, we defied the company supervisor's advice to solicit the corporation before asking anyone else for a gift. We met with representatives of the gift club to ask them to give $15,000 and then to pledge $15,000 each year for the next four years. Their commitment would total $75,000 and would permit them to commemorate the pediatric center of the hospital as a gift to the community by the employees' gift club.

A committee of employees, most of them parents, managed the gift club. They had already expressed a concern about the availability of children's services in the proposed hospital. We showed them plans. We invited them to discuss their concerns with a pediatric physician on the fund raising committee. At last, the employees were convinced, and they agreed to contribute $15,000 a year for five years, for a total of $75,000. We then worked with employee leaders of the gift club to urge the corporation to give $100,000 to bring the gift to our $175,000 target. Although the corporation did not announce its gift of $100,000 until the week after the campaign was completed, it carried us to our goal and helped us meet the awesome matching requirements of a sizable federal capital challenge grant.

Was this approach scientific? No, just a delightful commonsense equation: parents love children, parents will protect their children, and a modern pediatric facility will touch parents' interest. Moreover, the outcome satisfied everyone concerned: the corporation, the employees' gift club committee, the board of the proposed hospital, and the residents of the surrounding communities eager to have a health care facility in their region of the county.

Is fund raising a science? No, fund raising is mostly an art, a series of jigsaw puzzles, or entertaining problems, or delightful chess games. The art in this case was to ascertain the needs and *wants* of the principal constituents—donors, trustees, families, and children—and then to act accordingly.

It must be emphasized that fund raising requires a great deal of attention from the practitioner, whether she or he is endeavoring to orchestrate an annual fund for a small human services agency or to direct a major capital campaign for a large university. There can be no casual, "Tomorrow will do." That delay may invite another delay, and eventually the weight of these tomorrows will fester and cause you to lose that precious moment that would make a difference in the pace of the campaign.

Perhaps a thank-you letter is delayed, a mass mailing is not completed and is not delivered to the post office at the right time, or an opportunity is missed to talk with a key trustee or with a knowledgeable businessperson able to give you strategic information about closing an important leadership gift. Casual attention to details, inept listening, yielding to distractions and missing quiet hints, all will take their toll, weakening the fabric of the campaign and threatening the science of your plan.

Fund raising is more than disciplining the mind, compelling it to take and to maintain command of the minutiae of the fund raising campaign from beginning to end. There is also an art to giving total attention to those activities that make a difference in the solicitation of the major gifts that will inspire other donors to give at the required level. It has been said again and again in fund raising circles: give your full attention to those critical details that will make the difference between success and failure in your program. Be focused and, yes, even selfish. Direct your energy to those activities that will help you achieve your mission. Shun all distractions like the plague. The taste of success is sweet. The taste of failure is bitter—and it lingers.

Fund raisers must take the wisdom of leadership (art) and apply it to management and administration (science). We must understand what values have earned our focus. We must use the applied arts of philosophy, psychology, anthropology, sociology, and theology in creative understanding of people's interests and concerns, of their motivation for caring and sharing, and of their unselfishness and pride as they invest in benefits to others.

Structure as an Art

Fund raising relies on the building of a structure. The building blocks are analysis, planning, execution, control, and evaluation. Analysis and evaluation are sciences. In between them comes the art. The genesis of fund raising demands serious thought before a plan can be reduced to writing. Every practitioner should keep in mind the axiom, "It's what you do up front that counts."

Step 1: Analysis

Analysis is diagnosis, the process of discovery, the thoughtful examination of each element that will influence the planning and thus affect the outcome of the fund raising program. Certainly, analysis will serve to set the strategy in place. It is essential for the planner to study the intricacies of the nonprofit's environment in order to understand its scope and its tendencies to inhibit or to stimulate progress. Data analysis invites the pesky questions and compels hard answers. Critical thinking demands study of valid data that reach out to the marketplace. With this information at hand, energy can be directed to finding thoughtful responses to the following key questions that I have compiled over forty-six years of fund raising experience:

- Are the organization's mission and vision the driving forces for this fund raising program or is the focus simply that "the organization needs the money for its budget"? Budget fund raising will not arouse the passion of the potential donor.
- Is the chief executive supportive and willing to participate in the solicitation, or is her or his theme song, "But I thought that was why we hired you"? Will board members join the executive in singing that theme song or will they commit to give and to get? Fund raising limited to staff efforts is cold fund raising. The commitment of volunteer leaders brings a passion to the solicitation.
- Has the goal been tested against the real potential, or is it a reckless guess, an imposition by an uninformed executive or development committee? Goals must be able to survive a reality test. Have valid prospects been identified for those crucial top-level gifts? Focus your solicitation on reality, not on false dreams.
- Is the development office budget adequate to the task? Are there sufficient supporting staff to ensure that proper energy and time can be applied to working the plan? Penny pinching here may be expensive.
- Is the development staff knowledgeable about the organization's constituency? Has the constituency, or an important part of it, made its feelings known—its likes, dislikes, preferences, desires for recognition or for satisfaction? Be a boundary spanner. Get to know the needs and wants of your stakeholders.
- Does the donor base reflect sufficient excitement in the matter of donor numbers and gift quality to justify a goal increase for the year ahead? Are there sufficient potential givers at the right gift level to validate prospects for the pacesetting gifts? Do not stagnate. Anticipate future needs.
- Are there sufficient dedicated volunteers to champion the effort, to assume the responsibility to give, to solicit gifts, and to recruit additional volunteer solicitors?

All these questions are part of the analysis agenda, that critical examination of available data that will ensure that the institution is in line with its constituents—all those who may have a stake in the organization and may be able to affect its viability.

Step 2: Planning

Planning is the natural next step. The analysis of the comprehensive data will initially dictate the course to follow in the design of the fund raising plan. However, the heart and the mind should operate in balance when it comes to planning. Emotion and hard reasoning too often meet in combat, and this is destructive in the planning process. When the heart rules, certain decisions will be made that may pose difficulties later on. When reason alone rules, the passion inherent in the cause will be neglected, and the program will lack that touch of daring that motivates volunteers and injects excitement into prospective donors' souls.

Moreover, the mood of the environment in which the organization must function may well dictate decisions that do not please the planners. Yet it would be foolish to ignore strictures imposed by the prevailing culture.

Step 3: Execution

From analysis to planning to execution is the campaign's natural flow. The plan is in place. Activity must get underway. The trap here is to delay a planned activity. "Tomorrow, and tomorrow, and tomorrow,/Creeps in this petty pace from day to day," warned Shakespeare (*Macbeth* V.v.19–20). And the warning was an apt one. Initiative is stifled. Opportunities are lost. The pace of the program is slowed by indecision and delay.

Enthusiasm builds when the pace is fast. The energy level of volunteers and staff members remains high. It behooves the fund raising director to move the program along at a quick pace to prevent the energy lag that deadens campaigns and dampens the enthusiasm of staff and volunteers. A tight yet reasonable schedule is needed to keep enthusiasm at a steady pace. Make the campaign a party, a celebration. Encourage individuals to be happy and to have fun.

Step 4: Control

The next step is to control the fund raising campaign. Never let it get out of hand. The fund raising director must bear the responsibility for keeping the campaign on schedule and accomplishing the final result. The board chair, the chief executive, the development committee, and the volunteer chair of the campaign should not dictate the pace of activity once the campaign is in motion. These important leaders can confer with the director, can suggest a change of pace, and may even try to impose a schedule change. A wise professional will listen thoughtfully to their counsel and then make the decision that will serve the effort best. If the command position is relinquished and the director loses control, bedlam will erode the discipline, and problems will occur.

An example of what happens when control is lost occurred during an important capital campaign that I was directing as fund raising consultant in a midsized city in the Southwest. The pace had begun to lag, and volunteers were not sufficiently committed to the campaign. They resisted training. They were slow to give. Some never gave. They were not attending to their assignments. Once that occurred, further trouble lost no time arriving. A volunteer leader, who had indicated to me several times that he thought he knew much more about fund raising than I did, asked one of the office secretaries for a handful of blank solicitation gift cards.

The secretary, ignoring procedures, handed twenty blank cards to him, and he, in turn, distributed them to friends and requested that they solicit anyone they knew. He imposed no control, put no names on the cards, made no suggested gift levels—just told these people to go and ask. What happened next was inevitable. People who did not know the campaign strategy and were unaware of the prospect assignment procedures casually approached individuals to ask for insignificant gifts.

In this process, they capriciously approached several of our most important prospects, some in the potential $25,000 to $50,000 gift range, to ask them for $100. Follow-up solicitation of these prospective givers was difficult, to say the least. Damage repair was complicated and painful. Thus, I repeat the advice: never lose control of your campaign.

Step 5: Evaluation

Taking the last step and evaluating your progress at regular intervals is essential to the progress of your fund raising activity. Your operating plan should include benchmarks that enable you to draw conclusions about the progress being made.

One way to establish benchmarks is through the use of gift range charts, which, as described earlier (see Table 1.1), enable the fund raising director to compute gift numbers and gift sizes necessary to the successful completion of the campaign. A wise fund raising director will also prepare a version of the chart that substitutes names for numbers of prospects (number of prospects and gift levels will vary according to the size of the goal). Names can be assigned for solicitation purposes; numbers cannot. Periodic review of solicitation progress in the prospect name column will create a priceless information bank for the professional.

In addition, the development director will feel more secure in the progress of fund raising knowing the answers to these benchmarking questions. How many prospect solicitation assignments have been made? Are volunteers carrying out their solicitations? How many solicitations have been completed? How many gifts have been received? How many gift refusals have been reported? Are we on target with the plan's schedule? If not, what damage control is required? What follow-up will be required? Are we in line with our budget projections? Basically, these evaluation questions ask, Are we on target, ahead of the target, or behind the target? Can we project goal accomplishment at this pace? Is an immediate meeting with our leadership imperative to consider an alternate strategy that will change the course of this campaign?

In this way, the fund raising director pauses to take the pulse of the campaign, just as a doctor or a nurse takes the pulse of a patient at specified intervals. Many times, such control through periodic evaluation has saved the lives of campaigns I have directed.

When the campaign comes to an end, after the victory has been celebrated, it is time to evaluate the accomplishment in its entirety. This is an important assignment, a strategic stocktaking when campaign memories are fresh in the mind in order to prepare for the next fiscal year's activity. A program just completed holds a wealth of information, and this richness should be recorded for use as a measuring stick against the next fund raising effort. Who performed well among staff and volunteers? Who did not perform according to expectations? What remedial action is required before launching the next program? Was the research used to compile the gift range chart on target? Were gifts secured as specified by the gift range chart? Was the working timetable realistic? Did the campaign stay within budget or exceed budget? Was the communications plan well devised? Was it an effective instrument to help ensure our market position? How can the information from this campaign be used to plan a better annual fund program, special event, capital campaign, or planned gift solicitation? What changes will have to be made next year?

The closing evaluation exercise provides the fund development officer with priceless planning data for next year. That is one consideration. Another consideration is that once the development office uses these data to take stock of the team's production during the current year, the resulting information will prove an impressive tool in the continuing effort to orient (or, more bluntly, to educate) the executive staff, program and support staff, board of trustees, development staff, and development committee to the realities of fund raising on a continuing basis. Such "education" should not be seen as an effort to boast about achievement or justify failure. Instead, the data form an objective exhibit that explains the dynamics of a fund raising effort and the functioning of campaign components under different circumstances. What makes campaigns succeed and what makes them fail? Post-campaign evaluation is a learning experience, an adventure in discipline.

One of the chief fund raising officer's roles is that of a teacher. As such, she or he must always take advantage of an opportunity to explain fund raising to others and to persuade, cajole, and induce them to take fund raising seriously, according it the respect that it merits.

Conclusion

In the process of thinking and writing about science and art in relation to fund raising, I have convinced myself that fund raising is not solely art or science. It is an intriguing blend of the two disciplines, although more art than science. Science plays a key role. We need the skills of system management, data analysis, and critical thinking as we apply the wisdom of leadership in management and administration. However, fund raising results from an endeavor of art, in which we shape a wealth of knowledge from philosophy, psychology, anthropology, sociology, and theology into a creative understanding of donors and their reasons for giving.

Chapter Eleven

Language and the Gentle Art of Persuasion

If we listen to the cynics, we will hear that the language of fund raising is the language of manipulation, the language of coercion, the language of seduction, the language of the huckster. Is it not fortunate that philanthropic fund raising has been able to survive the ages despite the varying blotches planted by its detractors that have besmirched its garments?

Fund Raising as Begging

When fund raising had its start millennia ago, little energy appears to have been spent compiling a lexicon for its activities. Redmond Mullin's *Wealth of Christians* (1984, p. 161), as discussed in Chapter Nine, chronicles the activities, events, conflicts, and accomplishments underlying our emerging fund raising operation—which borrows from Greek, Roman, Jewish, and to some degree, Native American and other cultures—noting contradictions, mischances, and accords. In medieval times and after, money raising was generally depicted as begging. Funds were received primarily by the church in response to sales, fairs, soliciting letters and house-to-house calls, sermons, alms giving, and the sale of plenary indulgences and were directed to charity, to hospitals, and to church needs. Mullin's research unearthed the fascinating fact that Pope Urban II used indulgences as an inducement for men to join the First Crusade (A.D. 1096–1099). Those who died while on the crusade, according to the indulgences, were considered to have been absolved of sin by the church. Thus, it was believed that it was not necessary for them to pass through Purgatory on their journey to Heaven. Could it be acknowledged that this was the first recorded donor recognition plan!

Perhaps the first effort to define fund raising formally occurred in 1536 when King Henry VIII of England issued the *Act Against Papal Authority* and the *Beggar's Act,* stipulating that "every preacher, parson, vicar, curate of this realm should use sermons and other occasions to exhort, move, stir and provoke people to be liberal, and bountifully to extend their good and charitable alms and contributions from time to time for and toward the comfort and relief of the said poor, impotent, decrepit, indigent and needy people" (Mullin, 1984, p. 163).

Just short of a century later, the vocabulary of fund raising as begging and alms giving and, to a major degree, the techniques of fund raising, began to change with the arrival of the Puritans on the shores of the New World, and they continued to change as the centuries prodded and sometimes coerced fund raisers to strive toward professionalism. Yet some of the hubris of the donors of earlier centuries followed the art form of fund raising to the newer, greener pastures and some of the old language lingered on, as reflected in the title of Smith's "Honorable Beggars," which describes fund raising entrepreneurs in the United States during the seventeenth and eighteenth centuries in this country. However, companion titles for these fund seekers were springing up, too: "middlemen," "agents," "promoters," and the more pleasant term "fund raisers" itself.

But while we may prefer the term fund raiser, is beggar as bad as we might think on first hearing it applied to fund raisers? Smith (1968, p. 223) tells the tale of a young man preparing to ask John D. Rockefeller for a gift. Humbly, he said, "You do understand that I am not a beggar, Mr. Rockefeller." To which the great philanthropist responded, "I am sorry to hear that." Rockefeller relished the process of asking and did not consider the word begging to be depreciating.

The words bequeathed to us by our early pioneers as they plied their trade are not pejorative. Beggar was a forthright way to describe someone who asked for gifts.

Military Metaphors and Levels of Command

Other words that came into the fold during the late nineteenth century tended to clothe fund raising in a militaristic garb. These words emerged during the period that the outstanding fund raisers Charles Ward and Lyman Pierce converted fund raising from a medley of unrelated happenstances into a disciplined matrix (see Chapter Nine). It would seem logical that these two fund raising veterans, their mettle tested and proven in the "battles" of fund raising, should use the term "campaign" when they enlisted among the earliest professional fund raisers. Campaign was an apt title, they thought, to describe an intensive effort with tight timetables and tight controls. Volunteers recruited and marshalled into disciplined ranks of canvassers added to the aura of a tightly managed working team, a campaign army.

Some of this nomenclature with militaristic overtones still persists in fund raising today. A major fund raising effort is still identified as a campaign. A campaign has to have a chair (or "general") as the overall leader. The chair has to have associate chairs ("colonels"), to break down the command into manageable units. The associate chairs need "captains" to head the district teams ("battalions"). And these captains must recruit associates ("lieutenants") to head up the local teams ("squads").

The idea of organizing by levels of command has been critical to today's successful fund raising. We also talk about our "targets," our "heavy artillery" (brought to bear on targets representing big gifts), and our hardworking "foot soldiers," the volunteers who have to be "recruited," "trained," and "disciplined" and assigned to units and targets. They must "march" to the music of the mission and perform their duties with dispatch if they want to keep their "stripes."

Pierce and Ward employed military metaphors as they designed the strategies that made it possible for them to plan, launch, and operate a campaign and reach the campaign goal within a time frame never before achieved. The militaristic chain of command handed down the orders, defining targets, goals, timelines, volunteer recruitment needs, and checkpoints for evaluating progress and adjusting strategy if necessary. The militaristic structure and the discipline required to carry it out are still in vogue to a major degree in our era.

Military metaphors need not be intrusive to communicate an urgency and a need for efficiency to program planners. However, they send an eloquent message that discipline must rule if the program is to succeed. The military nomenclature frames the plan and quickly converts the concept to structure.

How to Describe the Case

The case, the justification for gift support, speaks of values and ought to be presented to the community in persuasive, vivid, sometimes almost poetic phrases to emphasize the urgency of the human or societal need and the potential of the working plan to resolve or at least palliate that need. The case is a hardworking tool that endeavors to communicate convincing thoughts, good ideas, a commitment to values, and descriptions of worthy plans and programs designed to address the concerns that justify the fund raising activities.

Rarely should the case be beseeching, and never exaggerating, condescending, coercive, or so arrogant as to project the idea that the responsible prospect has no other choice but to give. This approach rarely produces gift funds, but it is an efficient agent for alienating potential donors.

In addition, there are a number of specific harsh phrases, representing inappropriate and callous thoughts, that professional and volunteer fund raisers should avoid, both among themselves and when among their constituents. These phrases are anathema and merit a prompt dishonorable discharge from any campaign. Samples of such phrases, in common use today, are the following:

"I have to polish my pitch."

"I'm going to make a hit on good ole deep pockets."

"I'm going to back him to the wall."

"He's a lost duck. I've got him in my sights."

"She'll be on the hot spot before I finish with her."

"Let's tell them that it's for the kids. We'll use it for salary raises.
　Don't worry. They won't know."

"Give, get, or get off the board [or organization]."

"Let's hit the little old lady in tennis shoes."

"Give until it hurts!" (Why should it hurt? A better phrase is, "Give until it feels really good!")

"We're launching our annual budget campaign." (This phrase, lacking all passion for a cause, should have an indecent burial at sea.)

"Give to help us eliminate our debt." (The only person who will stir up some passion about this ask is the debtor.)

"It's that time again. Dig deep. We need it."

Conversely, it would be welcome if we could educate those who are outside fund raising organizations and do not understand them to avoid using derogatory names for us: "Let's face it. You're just a parasite" or "money grubber" or "money monger." "You're a professional pickpocket." "You're nothing but a huckster with gray suede shoes, aren't you?"

There are also good phrases to be considered, ones we should try to use more often. *Philanthropy* literally meant "love of mankind" to the Greeks who coined it. A commonsense phrase that should touch every person is "Giving is love." Giving that reflects concern for others is never to be represented as a burden, obligation, or responsibility. Giving is a privilege representing freedom of choice. No person should give under duress. Each gift should be an expression of gratitude by the giver for blessings received. Evangelist Dwight L. Moody in the late nineteenth century consistently appealed for love-motivated stewardship to raise money for schools and YMCA buildings. He raised thousands of dollars while preaching that "love must be the motive power. A man may give his thousands to the poor . . . yet if love does not prompt the deed, it goes for nothing" (Smith, 1968, p. 24).

The word *charity* has been abused, associated as it is so often with the unfortunate expression *do-gooders,* a derisive term. Yet the word *charity* is derived from the Latin *caritas,* meaning love, an act of goodwill or affection, giving that is not in disdain, and giving that does not impose a responsibility on the receiver.

There are other good words and phrases that should stand out prominently in the lexicon of the fund raiser. The phrase "values exchange," for example, which broadly defines the exchange that takes place between buyer and seller, can be a marketing tool for nonprofits. What values are exchanged when a donor makes a gift to a nonprofit? Fund raisers seem to have difficulty perceiving the importance of this question. A common answer is that the donor gets a tax deduction in return for the gift. But a tax deduction only *empowers* the gift. It is not the primary motivation for the gift. Consider the following values that donors receive upon making a gift, then discuss these concepts with friends and colleagues and try your hand at writing down the values donors receive:

Making a difference.

Becoming part of an important project.

Getting a warm feeling of satisfaction.

Having the privilege of giving back to one's community.

Reaching out to a person in need without that person's knowing that the donor is helping.

Having the feeling of joy that comes with gift making.

Achieving immortality when one's name is enshrined in a project.

Knowing that even though one cannot build a cathedral alone, one can contribute to make it possible.

Words That Define Critical Issues

The development staff, led by the director and supported by the chief executive and the development committee of the board, should give major attention to issues underlying these important terms: *relationships, stewardship, stakeholders,* and *accountability*. They call attention to a future that will be different in many different ways from our past.

Professional staff will have to be more aware of the market that surrounds them, more cognizant of the changing needs within that market, more sensitive to the changing attitudes and moods of the organization's stakeholders. Accountability is not just a nuisance buzzword. It is a day-to-day reality for nonprofits. Governments, corporations, foundations, and individuals are intensifying their demands for accountability from every nonprofit, as each has a right to do so. Those who are ready to demand accountability are not likely to give us unquestioned loyalty and that may raise concerns about the true stability of any nonprofit. The question is, Are you ready to respond to the new demands relating to relationships, stewardship, stakeholders, and accountability? Here are some specific questions to which we have to wrench thoughtful responses from ourselves and from the organizational conscience:

Are we aware of the interests, needs, and opinions of our stakeholders?

How can we improve our accountability so as to better merit the public's trust and to allay its concern?

How can we better hold the continuing loyalty of our donors?

Do we have a responsibility to learn as much as possible about what our stakeholders know about our mission and about the goals, objectives, and programs related to it?

How can we convince trustees that their support is needed during this era of increasing competition?

Do our thank-you letters and calls project sincerity, warmth, and true gratitude? (Or do they show boredom with the routine of it all?)

Do we check our donor base at regular intervals to study changes in giving patterns and practices?

How can we use these checkups to sensitize ourselves to the reality that donors are delightful people with whom we must have relationships (not simply cold electronic database entries to whom we can routinely send our five-year-old boilerplate thank-you letter, a letter completely devoid of any human passion or sign that the gift, regardless of its size, is truly appreciated)?

Do we try to use personal visits, phone surveys, mail surveys, and the like to learn more about our donors and their thoughts about us, our work, and our accomplishments in serving our clients?

Do donors think we have a down-to-earth dedication to the values articulated in our mission statement?

Do organize a one-on-one solicitation with each trustee? (Or do we just use mailings to ask our trustees to give?)

Do we play fair with our trustees by involving them in discussions of substance about programs, to help them understand how we are fulfilling our mission, goals, and objectives in service to our stakeholders, to immerse them in the soul of the institution, and to give them a feeling of being part of the mission in action? (Or do we just supply a cursory discussion devoid of passion and meaning, what Ivy League universities used to call "giving them a touch of the ivy"?)

Do we involve our executive, trustees, and development committee chair in convincing trustees to give and to solicit other prospects?

Does our mission statement reflect the dominant values our organization espouses? (Or is it a bald statement of goals?)

Do we wear our mission as a mantle when we seek to raise funds? (Or do we vest ourselves with the drab cloth of the budget?)

Do we honor the prospect by asking for a gift investment commensurate with her or his giving ability? (Or do we extend the tin cup when we ask, thereby demeaning the prospect?)

Do we proudly project the dignity of our mission and the pride of our work? (Or do we automatically apologize when asking someone to give?) The language of fund raising should broadcast pride, joy, privilege, mission, vision, values, passion, and integrity but never, never apology.

Fund raising is the gentle art of persuasion. Each person asking for gifts should go forth with pride and confidence in the work that she or he is doing and in her or his dedication to serving the public good. Here are two suggested approaches:

To a prospect. "We are hopeful that you will join with us in the advancement of this work. Your gift will make a difference." The prospect may say, "But I am able to give only $25. What kind of difference will that make?" Your truthful response can be: "Your gift combined with others that are being contributed will make a significant difference in our work. If $25 is the maximum amount that one hundred donors could give, those donors will supply $2,500 to support our work. If you can give more, we will be grateful for your generosity."

To a potential volunteer leader. "We can accomplish so much with these youngsters if this camp can be developed for them. I've been watching you as you work with the children, and I am impressed by your ability to draw adults into this program. I need your help. If I had your help, this camp could be completed by this time next year, and what a joy that would be to these youngsters. I do need your help; together we can do it." The words "I need your help" are as special as the words "I love you." They have the power to draw people to accept responsibility—particularly when people understand that the successful completion of a project will bring joy to the hearts of many. "I need your help" communicates a magic message: "You are a very special person. You are capable of accomplishing what many other people cannot. With you on our side, this job will be done."

Recall the inspirational words of Zikala-Sa quoted earlier: "Life is not worth living if it does not demand some little effort on our parts to contrive in it. It is not what we give for nothing, but what we inspire others to try or to do—that is the best, most valuable gift we can offer" (Joseph, 1995, p. 70).

It is within each of us to make a gift of ourself. Do it and celebrate the surge of gladness and pride in your entire system. You will understand how to reach out to people and how to give meaning to their lives. This is true philanthropy.

Conclusion

Words are our day-to-day working tools. They should reflect the importance and integrity of our work. They must give expression to our mission and vision, put conviction and integrity in our solicitations. Words are our links to our colleagues, our prospects, our donors, and our trustees and other volunteers with whom we work. They should be soft words, convincing words: "I need your help." "Your gift will make the difference." "Each of us is truly grateful for your generosity." "Your volunteer service is a shining grace." "Your dedication touches and inspires each of us." And that very special phrase, "Your generous gift will inspire us in our work, reaching out to help people."

Words can be wounding bullets or fragrant flowers. Karla A. Williams, principal of The Williams Group in St. Paul, Minnesota, says: "In all that we do, we must be ethical, above reproach. We must follow the strictest interpretation of the profession's code of ethics and take no action that would undermine the credibility of the institution or philanthropy itself" (personal communication, 1995). This injunction applies to our words as well as our deeds.

| My Start in Fund Raising

This chapter and the two that follow offer highly personal views of fund raising that may illustrate why many of us in this profession find fund raising more than just a job. One question has been asked of me often, in the classroom, during a consulting session, during a social gathering, or in a quiet conversation with a newfound friend. With an expression of incredulity, the person says to me, "How in the world, forgive me for being personal, but I have to ask, how in the world did you get into this business?" I have decided to answer that question here because of the many lessons my first major fund raising assignment contains.

From Public Relations to Fund Raising

In 1949, immediately after graduation from Syracuse University, I accepted a position with a public relations firm in Syracuse. One of the early assignments directed to me by my boss was writing print and radio news copy for the Upper New York March of Dimes, the local community chest and rescue mission, and a variety of other clients.

As I wrote news copy about the March of Dimes, I found myself thinking that marching dimes did not sound too exciting. As a matter of fact, in 1950, a parade of nickels and dimes was placed on the curbs of the main streets in Syracuse, but I was not too curious about them. President Franklin Delano Roosevelt, who had contracted polio as an adult, had put forth the idea of "all of the people of America" giving nickels and dimes to help fund research to try to eliminate polio from the face of the earth.

At the time, I knew nothing at all about some exotic bug with the fancy name of poliomyelitis, but it did not take me too long to find out that polio was a deadly, crippling disease afflicting children primarily and, to some degree, adults. I had asked my boss one day if I could devote some time to finding out what it was that people were marching for and why they were marching for dimes. I said it sounded like a waste of time. He responded, "It's not a waste of time. Go to the hospital, talk with doctors and nurses. Find out as much as you can about it." I went to the hospital. I listened. I asked questions. I learned, and I cried. I had seen casualties on battlefields in Africa and Europe during World War II. But I had never seen a sick child in an iron lung that helped the child breathe and stay alive. It was a brutal experience for me.

In the early summer of 1951, not long after my first visit to the hospital, the agency for which I worked was alerted to the fact that it would be assigned the task of planning and activating one of the first pilot programs to stage a Mothers' March on polio, raising money in Syracuse and the surrounding Onondaga County to expand poliomyelitis research. My education about polio was about to move in a new direction.

A representative from the national March of Dimes organization visited the agency for a briefing session with staff members. He explained to us that the March of Dimes fund raising activity at that time was producing from $15,000 to $18,000 from Onondaga County, and he told us, "Significantly more is needed if we are to protect our children from the scourge of polio." We talked for more than an hour about the details of the Mothers' March. "We will need special press support to help us recruit the numbers of volunteers needed to staff this effort. That will have to be part of your assignment. Are you prepared to put one full-time person in charge of this process," the visitor asked, "and if so, who is he?" The president of the agency turned to point at me. "Rosso will handle all of the details," he said.

My previous fund raising efforts had been directed to individual churches, Catholic and Protestant, in the county. I had no experience putting together and managing a countywide door-to-door campaign. My boss must have sensed my uneasiness because he winked at me and said, "I'll be here to help." Great! He had never staged or directed a fund raising program either, other than those associated with political campaigns.

Several days later, my boss and I had a daylong meeting with three political leaders, lifelong residents of Onondaga County. Our orientation to broad-scale planning was about to begin. Our three advisers brought maps of the county that detailed districts, wards, and neighborhoods for our edification. By the end of the day, our plan was reduced to paper and marked out on the maps for our continuing deliberations.

Campaign Planning

One of our first tasks had to be to recruit a Mothers' March chair, a community leader of the campaign. It was apparent that this person had to be a woman, and it was further obvious that the chairs of wards and blocks also had to be women. After all, this was to be a *Mothers'* March on polio. We needed to do some thoughtful research to identify the best candidates for these strategic positions. We made a series of telephone calls to the leadership of the local community chest, to the local archbishop, to Protestant and Jewish leaders in the county, to the mayors of each community in the county, to the editors of the daily newspapers, to the leaders of the chamber of commerce, and to the presidents of several social and service clubs. From these conversations, we produced a comprehensive list of key women throughout the county with reputations for performing in a leadership position whenever they accepted any community task. We appointed a general chair from this list. Within a week, she had formed her steering committee representing different areas of the county.

With this progress recorded, we decided to launch a countywide information program that we tabbed "Community Training to Wipe Out Polio—the Mothers' March on Polio." We also planned that the print media, both daily and weekly newspapers, would run major stories to alert the countywide community to the need for volunteers willing to help us organize and to solicit gifts in the neighborhoods. And we planned that training—informational sessions for all volunteers—would be simulcast by radio and television from 6:45 to 7:00 P.M. every Wednesday evening until the night of the march. Having written this in our operational plan, we then had to secure the cooperation of the print and electronic media. This was easy to accomplish, however, because they were aware that something needed to be done to halt the spread of polio and they were eager to help.

Once we had radio and television airtime and newspaper space promised, we had to write feature and news copy for each medium. Additionally, we needed a skilled commentator to give voice to the copy every Wednesday evening. We found a person with both a good voice and a good sense of humor to tell our volunteers, over the air, what they were supposed to do once the march was launched. He performed well.

We had a volunteer army building, its ranks reaching close to the one thousand mark. Control now had to be the key word and the key action to keep this monstrous locomotive on the track. We set weekly checkpoints, so we could ensure that the program was moving forward according to the planned schedule. Of course, the weekly simulcast was a boon to us. Through the reports of the ward and block leaders, we were able to record that a preponderance of volunteers were listening either to radio or one of the television channels for their instructions.

Having built this locomotive with about one thousand volunteers aboard, our plans for launching the action at the appointed time— 7:00 P.M. on a Wednesday evening—and receiving the results as soon as the action came to an end became important. We knew that print and electronic media would be eager to have the results as soon as the solicitation had been completed and the money counted.

Thus, as part of our plan, we visited with religious leaders to ask them to sound their church bells precisely at 7:00 P.M. on the appointed Wednesday. We met also with fire chiefs to ask them to sound all the sirens on their fire vehicles at the same time. We wanted to hear a bedlam of church bells and fire sirens that night, projecting broadly and loudly the message: "Polio! Start traveling. Your days are up here and throughout the world. Leave our children alone!"

In addition, news and feature stories were submitted to the newspapers. Special copy was prepared for the broadcast media, bulletins were sent to churches, and posters were put up throughout the county to alert the people. We had spread the word that people who wanted to donate should leave their porch lights on, and volunteers were told in the radio and television training broadcasts that a porch light was an invitation to ring the bell. A handkerchief tied to the doorknob of an apartment was also a signal that a volunteer had permission to ring the bell and ask for a gift. That evening, porch lights were on, and handkerchiefs festooned the hallways.

The Results

Reports from the wards and the blocks began to come in around 9:00 P.M. and continued until 11:00 P.M. The total money counted that evening was $80,000. More money trickled in during the weeks that followed. The two daily newspapers gave quite a bit of space to the march and to its conclusion, especially since the previous year's curbside parade of nickels and dimes had produced only about $15,000.

The following year, 1952, another Mothers' March on polio was staged, and a significant amount of money was contributed again. In 1954, Jonas Salk began testing the vaccine that became an effective weapon to virtually eliminate the scourge of poliomyelitis forever.

Lessons Learned

The first lesson is about planning. The incident that embodies the lesson took place during the 1952 Mothers' March, which was particularly memorable for me because of the way it ended. We had arranged to set up our control headquarters in a bank eager to attract possible customers. Starting at 9:00 P.M. on the day of the march, the ward chairs began arriving at the bank to drop off the money that had been contributed. Each chair had a sturdy bag to hold the money, and these bags were deposited in the bank foyer. We had some drinks and sandwiches for all who visited with us that night.

Around 10:30 P.M., the bank treasurer approached me to ask, "What are you planning to do about all of this?"

"About all of what?" I asked.

"About all of this money in those bags on the floor. I would imagine that it is at least $80,000 or more."

"What am I supposed to do with it?" I responded. "This is a bank. Aren't you planning to put it in safekeeping?"

"No money can be stored in here until it is counted and validated," the treasurer announced. "And since it is all in cash, you will need more than yourself to count it because two people have to sign the deposit card."

"Can't we use your counting machine?" I asked.

"No," he said, "it is locked for the night."

There seemed to be only one solution to this impasse. I slept with the money that night. I slept on the bags of cash. I have heard the phrase "hard money" many times, but this was the first time that I truly slept on it.

Here are some further, more general lessons that I garnered from my first major fund raising assignment.

Write a plan for the event by yourself. Give your draft to two or three people whom you trust. Ask them to write a critique of the plan and to return the critique to you. Consider their comments carefully.

If the plan has a timeline, rewrite it yourself in the form of a backward timetable, working mentally back from the event to the present, trying to anticipate and note down everything that might happen. I did that for the Mothers' March, and it saved us a number of headaches.

Meet with the general chair privately at least once a week to check progress, to exchange ideas, and to ensure that the program is moving on schedule.

Write a "what if" scenario in an effort to pinpoint any possible weakness in the plan and the actions that could be taken to eliminate that weakness. Be prepared as much as possible. For example, do not take it for granted that the banker involved will store your gift money for you. Make your own arrangements for that. I learned that people will be turned on if the cause is significant and the needs are valid.

I learned so many lessons during the time that I was planning, organizing, and directing a program of the scope of the Mothers' March. The importance of taking and maintaining control was a beginning and essential lesson. On a number of occasions, several businesspeople and a few professional volunteers tried to assert themselves to take charge of the project. I could not permit it because the instructions to me from the beginning were that "this is your assignment. You manage it no matter who asks, or tries, to take over." I had to learn how to take charge and to hold my position and, at the same time, not to alienate the community leader who wanted to set me aside. Fortunately, the chair of the steering committee supported me to the hilt.

As you conduct your fund raising activities, you will encounter the usual folks who want to tell you how to do, or not to do, certain parts of your program. Listen to them carefully, then make your own judgment about the action that should be taken. Moreover, when you listen to suggestions, do not try to make a yes or no judgment immediately. The idea you turn down in the morning you may want to reconsider in the evening when you are more relaxed.

Accept criticism gracefully. The critic may be a potential donor. Listen thoughtfully. Respond with, "That's an interesting concept. I'll have to think about it." I encountered some strong criticism during the first Mothers' March. During the days immediately before the campaign launch, I had visited the polio ward again, this time with a cameraman from one of the television stations who wanted to take some shots to draw attention to the fund raiser. One patient, a boy about eight or nine years of age in an iron lung, greeted the cameraman with a smile and a wave. He was a delight despite the constraints that held him tightly to the bed in the iron lung. He wanted to talk with us. His words had a staccato obedience to the rhythm of the lung. The cameraman and I listened carefully as the words came out: "My . . . mother . . . march polio," and he smiled. With the permission of the boy's mother and his doctor, the film of the boy saying, "My . . . mother . . . march polio" was used in a television news program, and it drew considerable sympathetic attention to the Mothers' March.

Did I pull criticism in my direction? Indeed I did. "Wrong, wrong, wrong!" people said. I heard that I was using truly unfeeling exploitation just to raise money from my friends, my neighbors, and my community. However, when I learned that across the nation a tremendous sum of money had been given to the cause of preventing polio and that the money was invested in the Salk vaccine research, I felt fulfilled. In our local campaign, the young boy injected a great measure of needed passion into the appeal.

Conclusion

Thousands of people across the nation who took part in the Mothers' March on polio earned the right to be proud. Today, poliomyelitis lacks its terror. I pray that that terror is lost forever.

I must confess that I felt very good about the accomplishment of those first Mothers' Marches, and I began to think seriously about fund raising. I debated whether I should join at that time the scant ranks of professional fund raisers or whether I should return to my first love, editing and publishing a weekly newspaper. When I learned about the impact that the Salk vaccine would have in our country and in my own family home, I set the idea of the weekly newspaper aside. I cast my vote to become a professional fund raiser. I never have regretted that decision.

Chapter Thirteen

Stewardship in Giving and Receiving

Stewardship is a reflection of many values critical to the practice of philanthropy and its working partner, fund raising. Stewardship is trust, responsibility, liability, accountability, integrity, faith, and guardianship.

Primarily, stewardship focuses on concern and respect for the needs and rights of those who give and those who receive, the constituents of the nonprofit organization. It is the conscience of philanthropy, a sentinel centering the organization on responsible action at all times.

It is fun occasionally to conduct impromptu sidewalk interviews, asking passersby to define philanthropy and stewardship. The responses I have received generally are posed as questions rather than answers: "An exotic insect?" "I know, I know. A new disease just discovered?" "Aliens from space not fully identified?" "People who serve you on airplanes or tour ships or trains?" "We got stewards in church, but we don't know what they do. Do you know?"

Advancement executive Daniel Conway, author of *The Good Steward* (1994), traces the meaning of *stewardship* from its Middle English and Old English stems (p. 10). According to the *Oxford English Dictionary, steward* is derived from the Old English *sti*, meaning "house" or "some part of the house," and *weard*, meaning "keeper" or "caretaker." Thus, the original meaning of *stiweard*, or *stigweard*, was "keeper of the house," an official who controlled the domestic affairs of the household and assumed the responsibility to keep the house in good repair.

Stewardship, as redefined in contemporary rhetoric, carries an even deeper burden of trust, responsibility, and accountability for proper management and administration of the resources charged to the person in a steward's stead. Within the context of contemporary nonprofit governance and management, the role of steward and its corresponding obligation of stewardship is seen to apply to any person in a position to manage or account for financial resources: trustees, the chief executive officer, the financial officer, and the development officer and other members of the fund raising staff. Essentially, stewardship is asked of any person in a sensitive position, one who can preserve or shatter the integrity of the entity serving the public good.

The attributes of stewardship as they apply to individuals were very much in the minds of community leaders during the pre-Revolutionary era. Cotton Mather, in his 1710 "Essay to Rich Men," expressed the responsibility this way: "Sirs, you cannot but acknowledge that it is the sovereign God who has bestowed upon you the riches which distinguish you . . . the riches in your possessions are some of the talents of which you must give an account to the glorious Lord who has entrusted you with them." Mather's thesis was that the Lord conferred upon "rich men" an obligation to use their gifts of talent, energy, and treasure wisely for causes that serve the public good, as a statement of gratitude for gifts bestowed (Smith, 1968, p. 24).

In the remainder of this chapter, I offer five tales, each with a message to help us accept the meaning of stewardship in philanthropy and fund raising today as something significantly different from the way fund raising is sometimes regarded, as a murky business, a sinister occupation that violates personal privacy with no sensitivity about the feelings of individuals approached for charitable gifts to support one cause or another.

The Littlest Big Gift

In the sixties, I was assigned by the George A. Brakeley fund raising consulting firm to direct a capital campaign to build a new hospital in Santa Clara County, south of San Francisco. It was a difficult assignment for a number of reasons not essential to this tale. In an effort to win support for this project, I conducted coffee klatches in many homes in the community to talk about the need for a hospital, to answer questions about the plan for the campaign, and to ask for acceptance and support.

The coffee klatches kept me awake at night, but they were effective in many different ways and particularly inspiring in one instance. A member of the hospital's board of trustees invited me to her home for a presentation to interested neighbors. The meeting was successful. Many intelligent questions were asked, and the mood was positive throughout. I noticed, as I presented my facts and appealed for the listeners' support, that the daughter of the board member, nine or ten years old, sat with the group and seemed to listen intently to my words.

After the coffee klatch was over, I stayed for a bit to talk to the board member about the meeting and the reaction of the group. During this discussion, the board member's daughter asked permission to interrupt in order to hand me an envelope. "This is from my piggy bank. I want to help build the hospital," she said, much to her mother's surprise and mine. The envelope contained $4.32. Yes, I remember it to this day. Philanthropy? By all means—it was one of the most selfless, most touching gifts of the campaign. Not precisely the widow's mite but certainly as significant, nevertheless. The thank-you letter to that child was lovingly crafted.

Giving with Joy

One lesson still etched in my memory was taught to me by a canon of an Episcopal cathedral during the final days of a major capital campaign to complete that cathedral's construction. He encountered me in a corridor and braced me with questions and comments.

"Aren't you a member of the campaign team?" he asked.

"Yes," I responded.

"You folks are doing this all wrong," he charged.

"I do not understand," I had to reply. "We are close to reaching our goal. The campaign will be successful."

"Success of the campaign is beyond the point," he countered. "You are not teaching folks to give properly. By focusing on such basic needs as nuts and bolts and construction costs, you are encouraging people to give from the bottom of their financial resources and not from the top. You are not teaching proper stewardship."

"How are we encouraging gifts from the bottom?" I inquired, in my naïveté. I had not heard the word stewardship before, and I was not aware of its central meaning or its implications.

"You talk of mundane things. These concerns are valid, of course. But they don't touch the soul of the person. They don't lift the spirit, and because they don't, they plead for gifts of convenience, for reluctant gifts, small gifts of little meaning to the donor. The donors give this moment. They will forget what they have done before the hour is gone."

"What is required, then?" I asked.

"There is no passion in your expression. You do not touch the depth of their souls. Explain the rare and glorious opportunity that is theirs to help build a cathedral. They cannot build a cathedral with their own hands. And yet they can be an integral part of this accomplishment simply by making a gift. A gift to the best of their ability. A gift that will bring joy to their hearts. A gift from the *top* of their resources. Don't foster reluctant giving. Reluctant gifts are urged by the mind. They depress the spirit. Ask them to make a gift prompted by the heart, a gift that will fill them with joy. These are gifts that are stimulated by the spirit. That is responsible stewardship, a truly generous gift, a gift from the top of their resources, offered with joy, meaning, and gratitude for the privilege of being able to make such a gift."

The canon went on to explain that responsible stewardship entails giving from the gladness of our hearts. Thus, we are giving of ourselves. We are expressing gratitude for all the gifts that we have received. By giving from the "top of our means," we are giving something of ourselves to the cause. This is true philanthropy, giving with joy in our hearts.

A Life Not in Vain

Two interesting news stories, captured from two different newspapers from two different cities on the same day, also add meaning to the word stewardship. One is an inspiring story of a dream fulfilled. The other is a poignant tale of a barren existence, devoid of any meaning.

The story of the dream fulfilled concerns a middle-aged postal clerk, the son of a sharecropper, earning $17,000 a year, who wanted to do something meaningful in his lifetime. Although his own education had stopped in the eighth grade, he gave $35,000 to a university to endow a scholarship fund providing $1,000 a year to two needy students, athletes of promise in both their academic and sports achievement. The $35,000 included his life savings and $13,000 that he borrowed in order to establish a fund that would assist two students. A development officer at the university tried to dissuade him from giving up all his savings, but he felt that his wants were simply satisfied, as long as he had the basics of food and clothing and shelter.

We tend to think of philanthropists as rich people. This tale directs us to another dimension of giving. It is the tale of a true steward, a man of limited financial resources but rich in spiritual resources. Truly, there is a joy in giving by anyone, rich or poor.

An Isolated Life

The second news story ends on an entirely different, pitiful note: "The W&W Food Market was closed Saturday night, a wreath of white roses hanging on the door." The story recounts how a fifty-seven-year-old man was found dead of natural causes on the floor of his home one Friday night in April 1979, amid trash piled five and six feet high in some places and enough money to fill sixteen garbage cans.

After the county sheriff's deputies had cleaned up the house, the actions of the man who had scattered several hundred thousands of dollars throughout his house were still a mystery. The money, in $10, $20, $50, and $100 bills, was in the bathtub, in trash cans, and on the floors. Coins were piled seven or eight inches deep. The money was mixed with trash on all of the floors. Uncashed checks filled boxes throughout the home. The man was the owner and manager of a food store, and neighbors reported that after his wife's death in 1973, he lost interest in society, devoted himself to work, and lived the life of a recluse. He was at the store whenever it was open, and although he greeted his neighbors as he was coming and going from work, he almost never stopped to chat and rarely had any visitors.

There are many tragedies in people's lives. Perhaps the most tragic is a lonely death in an empty house, a death unknown, a death unmourned. Stewardship has a deeper meaning than just giving cash. Puritan leader John Winthrop added a spiritual message to the concept of stewardship: "As members of the same body, we must delight in each other [and] make this concern our concern." Giving, receiving, and managing human and financial resources responsibly are all aspects of stewardship. It is sad that the store owner did not reach out.

Teaching Philanthropy to the Young

A continuing concern for our society is whether our young people will carry on our tradition of philanthropy. This tale of my two grandsons suggests that we can teach them the way. Gregory is seven. Christopher is five. Their weekly allowance is one dollar. Under the tutelage of their mother, each child distributes his allowance this way: twenty-five cents "carry around" money for things he wants to buy right now; twenty-five cents put away for items that will take some time to save for; twenty-five cents long-term savings for college; twenty-five cents for the government for necessary services.

When this last category adds up to $5 or $10 or more, the child can choose a charity to give it to. In a basic way, these children are beginning to learn about money management, an important lesson even at the tender ages of five and seven. Equally as important, they are learning that it is natural to give money away judiciously, as a philanthropic gift to projects and programs that in some way will contribute to the general quality of life, preserve and advance particular values, or touch a person in such a way as to ensure a better life ahead for that person.

Chapters of the National Society of Fund Raising Executives (NSFRE) have been active in working with groups of young people to generate awareness of philanthropists and experience in philanthropy. Under the program Explore the Spirit of Giving with Youth, young people select a project, pledge a minimum of $2,000, and raise $1,000 of the gift themselves. That $1,000 is then matched by the NSFRE Foundation from funds generated by a $20,000 challenge grant from the Kresge Foundation. INDEPENDENT SECTOR, a Washington, D.C. research, information, and service organization, reporting on a survey of continuing youth activity, stated in a press release on the projects that "if volunteering and giving habits of teenagers are an indication, the future support of America's charities and causes is bright."

The Significance of Gifts

I firmly believe that giving willingly, thoughtfully, and generously does bring joy and greater meaning to a person's life. Let us consider the situation in each of the tales about those who gave.

The young girl who gave $4.32 to the hospital campaign sat quietly during the discussion of the need to build a hospital. She heard the presentation. She listened to the questions and answers. She made up her mind. A case can be made that her small gift would not truly cover any part of the $5 million project cost, so why is her gift significant? Because she made her own decision. She decided that she wanted to give. It would have been sad to denigrate her offering, to set aside her wishes, to explain that the gift was inadequate. In my judgment, her decision made of her own free will matched the significance of the three-, four-, and five-figure gifts made by corporations, foundations, and a goodly number of individuals. They gave from discretionary holdings. She gave all she had in her piggy bank.

The deepest desire of the postal clerk who set up a scholarship fund was to prove that he had "not passed this way in vain." Was his a selfish, self-serving act, was he giving $35,000 to a university to extol his own virtue? The scholarship fund was named after him, but that was only appropriate. He gave his entire life savings and then borrowed $13,000 to add to that sum to set up a fund for the purpose of encouraging two student athletes to earn academic degrees not available to him. Did he pass this way in vain? Was he not a proper steward of the limited resources in his possession?

We might ask whether the university development officer was a responsible steward when he set aside his eagerness to add $35,000 to the university's scholarship fund and counseled the clerk not to give away his entire life's savings. The professional fund raising practitioner is servant to fund raising and by association, then, servant to philanthropy, serving it dutifully, with integrity, and with love for the good that this engrossing phenomenon can bestow on our society. Such stewardship is citizenship at its most meaningful level. The officer acted responsibly on behalf of the donor and the institution.

Did the cathedral canon offer cogent counsel to the young fund raising consultant? The stories in this chapter support his contention that giving should come from the top and not from the bottom of a giver's holding if the gift is to have significant meaning to the donor, making him or her aware of the rewards of stewardship.

Conway expresses this view eloquently:

> Stewards see themselves as God's agents, the caretakers of all they have and are. As a result, stewards develop a special reverence for life. They care for one another and for the civil society they serve. They strive to simplify their lifestyles; and in the very act of conserving things of this world, stewards realize a fullness and productivity that is creative, not destructive. That's why stewards are good money managers and good administrators. It is also why fund raising is successful, in the long run, only when the organization seeking funds is keenly aware of, and responsive to, its stewardship commission [1994, p. 27].

Nonprofits, meriting tax-exempt privileges under section 501(c)(3) of the federal tax code, inherit a trust to use wisely and accountably the resources entrusted to their care. These resources include both financial assets and human assets, such as clients, donors, paid staff, unpaid volunteers, and other constituents. Serious regard for this trust is the soul of stewardship.

If we accept the philosophy that stewardship flows from our common value system, then it is clear that ethical fund raising simply surfaces these values and illuminates them. That is why a sensitive presentation with an emphasis on *vision* and *mission* will supersede manipulation any day. Sincere passion reflecting the solicitor's commitment and respect for the purpose of the work and its meaning to the civic community will stimulate more interest and desire to give than any contrived maneuvering to induce the gift.

Nonprofit Stewards

The primary stewards of the not-for-profit organizations of our country have specific as well as general responsibilities of stewardship.

The governing board. When an entity organizes itself to qualify for tax-exempt status under state and federal law, the governing board, under the statutes, assumes the task of overseeing use of the financial resources dedicated to program advancement. It is generally said that the primary responsibility of a governing board is to hold the nonprofit organization in trust in the public interest to ensure that it functions according to its statement of mission. This can be a heavy duty for each member of the board. By taking their charge seriously, trustees become both servant leaders and stewards.

The chief executive. The chief executive projects the shadow of the organization over the landscape of its constituency. In this role, the executive becomes a steward, a guardian of the total quality of the organization's resources. A caring staff lengthens and strengthens that shadow.

The financial officer. If the organization has a financial officer, he or she becomes the custodian of the treasury, attending to its well-being and sufficiency on a day-to-day basis and ensuring that its riches are committed unrelentingly to the advancement of programs serving the mission. In this respect the financial officer is a steward.

The chief program person. The person in charge of a nonprofit program rivets the attention and the skills of the program staff to the proper planning and execution of programs that address the human or societal needs constituting the core of the mission statement. Program directors and staff are stewards because they are true servants to the mission and to the accomplishment of goals and objectives—generally a deed never completed because of the nature of the needs.

The chief development officer. The chief development officer and the development staff hold major stewardship responsibilities to communicate with, interact with, and involve and solicit the organization's constituents. The development officer serves as an advocate for the constituents inside the organization by representing their needs, their interests, and their concerns to management. He or she serves as an advocate for the organization in the larger community by explaining its mission, detailing programs related to that mission, reporting and justifying financial expenditures, and verifying fund raising goals as necessary to the work being done.

Conclusion

Fund raising is educating, teaching, nurturing, advising, and counseling donors; encouraging and assisting donors in achieving their philanthropic objectives. Integrity—that is, stewardship at work—is a guiding principle in helping donors invest their gift money in work of their interest, with the assurance that the philanthropic gift will be used judiciously in serving the public good.

The development officer, having worked hard to secure the gift, now must serve as a steward of the integrity of the organization while also keeping faith with donors, the executive team, the board, the staff, the volunteers, and the constituents being served. The development officer initiates the giving action. He or she must complete the transaction by prodding all, staff and volunteers, to close that action by assuring full accountability to the stakeholders. Stewardship is a special quality. It must be honored. It must be perpetuated through the work of the institutions of the independent sector.

Chapter Fourteen

Recollections by One Who Was There

One day, a copy of an aged book fell into my hands through the generosity of a friend who loves books as much as I do. The title was intriguing enough to take my immediate attention: *Recollections of a College Beggar by One Who Was There*. Certainly, with that invitation, it was difficult to set the book aside. Adding to the lure was the issue date of 1882. There was, however, no identification of the author and no identification of the publisher.

The language on the pages suggests that the author was a minister serving in the hire of churches and church-related colleges as a roaming fund raiser. I cannot identify the author otherwise. I can only provide his words, a voice from the past, when official "beggars," as they were called as I have explained earlier, trod miles and miles of rural landscape, soliciting funds for colleges, churches, and human services agencies. For the most part these beggars walked or rode a horse, pony, or a mule. They traveled by train only when they could afford it, which was rarely. They were the fund raising professionals of the eighteenth, nineteenth, and early twentieth centuries.

The book honored its title by pleading plaintively, "Please read me," when I first saw it. I submitted with curiosity and soon found in its story many memories of my own beginnings in Syracuse, New York, in the late 1940s, when there were no professional books, no fund raising workshops, no mentors, and limited expense accounts. Seat-of-the-pants teaching was the wisdom of that period. I walked the miles, also.

The remainder of this chapter reprints some passages from this old book, to introduce you to the agony and limited ecstasy of primitive fund raising in the previous century. How much was the person paid? Perhaps enough to buy a small hamburger and a glass of milk in this era. How long did the person work each day? Generally from dawn to significantly after dusk.

Today, when your computer is down, the mail is late in arriving, your airplane departure is delayed, your page proofs are not delivered in time, or your best prospect wants to demur, remember your professional ancestor of a century ago hurtling fences to avoid a charging bull. The long day is coming to an end but although he is tired and distraught, he still has five miles to walk or to ride a balking donkey in order to meet with an important prospect who eventually will plead poverty and will apologize that he cannot honor his invitation to dinner that night.

Here, then, are selected extracts from *Recollections of a College Beggar by One Who Was There.*

Introduction

"It is the object of these pages to give the reader an insight into the thoughts and experiences that came to me during two years in the field as a College Beggar. . . . We intend to select the humors and trials which have been mingled during the journey, and to make you feel as near as possible to some of the experiences that met us on the way.

"If we would know men better, and sympathize with humanity more, we should open our eyes to the different sides of human life, and thus have a better appreciation of the being who has come up from savagery and barbarism into his present condition. A right knowledge of the world will lead us to a more just estimate of humanity. With a clearer vision in viewing mankind, we shall not be as likely to be warped in our judgment concerning men and women. We shall learn to keep from either extreme."

Selfishness Versus Nobility

"These pages will show not only the selfishness and narrowness so commonly found, but also much nobility of character and generosity of soul, which show that this world is much better than most people think.

"For in our walk through life, we notice many an illustration of self-sacrifice in humble hearts and homes, remembered with peculiar fondness by the Great Spirit. We, of course, do not find many Peabodys, Girards, and Buchtels.

"It is rare that willingness and ability are so well blended; for wealthy men in their search after riches are apt to form habits that check the spirit of liberality. But few realize what a noble thing it is for a rich man to rise above those habits and exercise a heart and hand of generosity. It is a happy thought that the world is improving in this direction.

"But while we regard with so much honor those men of large means, who have bestowed their bounty on public institutions, we do not want to forget those many people in the more humble ways of life who have shown a nobility of mind and purpose of soul at which the angels above might look with profound admiration. And while we bestow such praises upon the rich for the bounty of their benevolence, we should not be unmindful of those who in a quiet way have shown a spirit equal to those whose praises are on so many lips.

"What have these two years (wandering the landscape as a College Beggar) presented to our view? Perhaps it may at least create a little sympathy for that class of people known as tramps, and more especially for the one who has tried to serve humanity in the capacity as a College Beggar.

"The first field where my labors were, one would think, might be quite productive; but after several days of hard work, riding and walking under the burning sun, using all the arguments and persuasions at my command, my conclusion was that this world is anything but a bed of roses. The thoughts and feelings that went through my mind, it is hardly wise for me to tell; but those whose brains are active, can no doubt, imagine not a few of the emotions which my soul underwent, after laboring faithfully day after day, without meeting the amount of success which my hopes had painted . . . but not many days' experience taught me what was a good thing to learn, that it is much easier to be liberal with other people's money than it is to get them to be so."

Visiting the Book of Remembrance

"The first section that I visited is on my 'Book of Remembrance,' and as long as my memory endures, the record of those days will stand. From what has been said you must not conclude that my work was not fruitless there. According to my conceptions, my expectations were not realized. But there is an old Greek saying: *arche de toi emiste pantos,* which means 'the beginning is half of the whole,' and it may apply to a work of this kind no less than to the study of Greek. The hardest part of anything is the beginning of it.

"A lesson learned: Getting used to the work, and getting a good headway are good points gained, and because results did not come in so large a way as I hoped, I learned to take the matter coolly and trust to time for results. In this work, as in other work, seeming failures are often seeds of a greater success by and by.

"In this territory, I found one man who reads much and keeps well posted in the affairs of the world. He went almost into raptures in expressing admiration for a man who had given so largely to educate humanity; and yet our admiring friend did not admire enough to suit me. Perhaps if he will continue to admire he will reach the point which he ought to see. I hope my friend will not wait too long, and if he or anyone like him, should see these remarks let him give them a prayerful consideration. Let the fire burn in their hearts.

"Two years after my visit to this man, I saw him again and he was still holding the matter open—waiting. The great trouble with men is that they are so slow in deciding.

"Decision of character is a grand thing. Decision of action is also grand. Others there are who are waiting, and we hope they will not wait too long.

"It is cooler weather and we feel more like prosecuting the work of begging. I call it *work,* for if anything requires labor, it is pegging away at men for cash. Many people will keep you overnight and gladly entertain you for days at a time, when they cannot be induced to pay out money. The reader is aware that people are more willing to feed tramps than they are to give their money, but then one after the description of the writer no doubt would have somewhat more easy time in that direction than those who are considered less worthy.

"We explored new fields and found reward for our trouble in some cases, and in others the reward is yet to come. A few miles beyond, I paid my compliments to a man who had no less than thirty-three hundred acres of fine land, six thousand sheep and other stock in the same proportion. He opened his heart to me, and increased my list, giving me encouragement for greater expectations in the future; and should he come across what is here printed, let him bear in mind that he is remembered, not only for what he has done, but in hope that a handsome endowment may yet bear his name. On this man's brother, I tried to make an impression, but for his *lift* [colloquialism for *gift*] we are waiting until he is *shaped*, and we trust he will be in that condition soon."

You Rub Our Back, We'll Rub Yours

"Upon arriving at a new destination, we found that attempts before had been made in the interest of this College, and that a short time before an agent had been induced to postpone the canvass in that place until more favorable weather. On my introduction they invited me to postpone my attempt in that direction, as they had a debt of their own to remove, and they did not know how it was to be done. After a somewhat lengthy talk on the question, they told me if I would raise their own church debt for them, they would give the College a lift.

"I went to work and cleared away every dollar of their burden, and they had quite a sum extra. But now they thought it best for me to give them another call for my college purpose, and so, I yielded to their advice.

"I waited a few months before undertaking this work with them. On reaching the place at about the time signified, some of those who had encouraged me to put off my canvass had just as many excuses as they had on my first visit, and I think more. But I had made up my mind that I should not be put off any longer, but go forward and do my part here in relation to the College. Of course, these men, under the circumstances, hated to refuse me, although some of them wished that I had kept away.

"Finally, most of them did something to aid me, some of them not as largely as I desired, but I was thankful that they concluded to put me off no longer and, on the whole, I was encouraged.

"It is not rare that we find those who are full of insinuations, and get out of our hands before we are aware. In a certain place I had the promise of an answer the following morning, but I was disappointed and vexed in learning that he had started off early that day with his dinner pail. He knew that I expected to go away that morning, and I thought he intended to slip out of my hands. I made up my mind that I would find him before I left that town. And so with a speech fully prepared to deliver to him, I started with a small boy and rig. It was not for the money that I was making this journey, but for the satisfaction of giving him a piece of my mind. But on the way my better nature began to work, and I concluded that I would turn this trip into profit, if possible. So by the time that I reached him, my vinegar had been placed out of sight, and I showed the sweeter side of myself to him.

"It so happened that he was touched just right, and responded to my call without urging. So by overcoming myself I won a double victory. It may be that it was well that I secured his subscription in this place, for it is not impossible that domestic objections would have prevented my success with him nearer home.

"A few miles' drive brings us to another small town, where we view the sights. The prospects are by no means grand. We find one man who needs more than he has, and we do not inflict on him any pain.

"Another by a little extra pressure would no doubt have done something, but I thought if I had been he I should have declined, and so I let him go. Another man received my attention a little while, but he had so much grumbling to do that I decided to have a little combat with him and leave him alone. Perhaps if his stomach had been in a better state he might have been rich enough to have aided me.

"Only one man in this town added to my money strength, and it cost a whole day to secure the small sum which he bestowed. Not that he required much urging, but there being no other work near, I waited for him to return from a visit several miles away. It is well here to say that each encounter is a lesson in frustrations and forbearance.

"I plod along the weary way. Wheat fields are before me. Meadows and cornfields come in my way. Fences have to be climbed, ditches crossed, gates opened, bars taken down, mud waded, and other difficulties encountered.

"Such tramps as these to find our victims give us the secret as to why our beloved parson here prefers to remain at home in the stillness of his study.

"It is much easier to do these things in *theory* than it is to do them in *reality*. It is much harder to dig for the prizes of this world than it is to dream about them.

"When one goes out in the rain, or under the burning sun, and travels all the way until he becomes tired and sore, it requires no small amount of spirit to do the work generally needed to induce a man to give away his hard-earned dollars. And yet such is what we must do if we would make our mission a success. And if at any time a person needs hope, it is while he is going through the trials, the hardships and difficulties of a college beggar.

"Many people are so constituted that the first refusal will put the damper on any further aspiration that they might have had, and they will switch the track and put their engines in another direction. But one of the first things that we should learn is the *great need of grit*. Whatever may be one's mission, whatever the work he has before him, he must remember that any great purpose cannot be realized without much "push" and "a firm hold of the object" before him. Only such a spirit will bring the result for which we labor."

The Spirit of Pluck and Nerve of Patience

"In this work of raising money . . . the spirit of pluck and the nerve of patience are especially needed. And I apprehend that these two qualities are about as useful as everything else. In fact, if one is unwilling to wear out shoe leather and to do any talking, he should never undertake the labor of reaching the purses of his fellow-men. Now, the writer of this work never claimed to be a *great* Christian; he never considered himself as too pious, and yet he has tried in a humble way to live about square in his general deportment, and he has never imagined himself not a bad Christian. But when he began to encounter the difficulties of the world as realized in his experiences as a College Beggar, he learned things about himself that were before unknown to him.

"He found it was much easier being calm and sweet in temper when in the quiet of his library or among selected people than it is to preserve a tranquility of soul while coming in contact with the sharp edges of human life, such as we find exhibited in our walks among the various phases of society. It was not long before I was convinced that my work was not one to be envied.

"After driving a short distance, I called at a place to see one whom I considered a good subject for my business, but lo! and behold! he was not to be found, he had gone away on a trip that day and he could not be seen.

"Going on somewhat further, and seeing a 'warm friend' of the faith, I made another 'try.' He is genial in his talk, takes you tightly by the hand and one would think, 'here is the good place where my soul will be made glad.' But, although he is such a strong adherent to the cause of his church, he is 'too poor' to give to anything that goes beyond his own community, notwithstanding the fact that he owns a beautiful home, a large farm, and ticking notes in his own pocket.

"It's too bad there are so many people of that description. To hear such a person you might be induced to raise a fund to keep him from starvation. One would think, to listen to the grumbling stories of poverty in homes where the piano sends forth lovely tunes, or where pictures of beauty hang on the walls of the finely carpeted rooms, that all is not in this world as the appearance would seem to show.

"A beautiful home is a joy and a charm. But a soul filled with thoughts of benevolence is a grander thing to contemplate than any of the 'externals' of the world. Could these narrow-sighted people be forced for a little while to be denied the comforts and many of the necessities of life, which are wanting in so many homes of sorrow and poverty, they might exercise more gratitude for the fortune which has favored them?

"But we find in this world men with every comfort and luxury that money can buy—with mansions of stone, lovely lawns, rich carpets and furniture of the most costly kind and splendor, and yet it is often they lack certain things which are so needful in filling the measure of a man's being. They lack that spirit that reaches beyond the narrow circle of self and home to comfort and bless mankind.

"It is not because this man of whom I spake did not answer my special call that he appears to me in the light that he does, for many noble-minded men have I met who did not deem it best for them to put their means in this particular direction, but the little exhibitions which cannot here be described, showed him to be lacking in some of the important requirements of human life."

The Compensation of a College Beggar

"It is well enough to here say that the writer preached the Gospel in many places where a congregation could be assembled. And in some of them there is still a need of that kind of work, for when I tell of my experience in this line, on some of the tours, the reader may understand why it is that so many people prefer a different calling.

"Ministers are considered by some as being different from other people. Perhaps they are in some things. But however that may be, they are like the rest of the world in other respects. They are obliged to eat and although they may not imbibe so freely as some, they must also drink, and under the present condition of things, they are in the necessity of having a place where they can cover their heads, and a place to shelter their family—not to say anything about the company that must necessarily receive the hospitality of their homes.

"If a minister manages to become the owner of a horse and buggy he must have hay and grain to feed his horse, or else he will have to sell, give away, or kill the animal. And when ministers are compelled to travel by trains or trolleys on their duties, the company does not often treat them as 'dead-heads,' but although their fares are reduced in some cases the extra amount of riding will make the ministers' railroad expenses far exceed the average patrons of that institution.

"Not only are the above things to be considered, but a minister and his family are obliged to have something to wear, and it is not a sin for him to have a little regard for the future, that when he becomes unfit for his work he may not be an object of charity.

"It may be that in the cases before us the people imagined that because I was laboring for a College they could have my services for free. But the College did not pay me when I was not at work raising money, and although I was presumptuous enough to present the claims of a College or any worthy object outside of myself, I could not often muster the courage to tell my hearers of my individual needs.

And so, often while wishing that they might themselves be thoughtful enough to make good my extra time and expenses, I was just too timid to be just to my own requirements. Thus I went away with less money than I had before starting out to fill the appointment.

"Here is an example of the level of generosity that I encountered when I dared to make reference to my own needs:

"The drive to the destination was a long 80 miles with horse and buggy. I arrived there in time, and preached my sermon to a good audience in a certain place where wealth was plenty. I got up courage to mention the fact of my own needs to one of the leading men of the parish, and said if the friends would like to chip in I should be thankful for their kindness.

"I noticed nothing further that day, until just before I started away from the man's house he took out a dollar and gave it to me, and said that he was unable to do more. The fact, it appeared, was that he was troubled with the diffidence and paid the small amount himself.

"I made another long drive of many miles, and, I had a large audience at the next place, only one man was thoughtful enough to give me a little to help lubricate the wheels. These same people wanted me to preach again.

"During the trip to meet these two engagements no less than four days of my time were taken from my regular business, and several hotel bills for myself and charger went to make up the cost of that occasion. The wear and tear of horseflesh, horseshoes and buggy added to the other expenses led me to think that I was not coming rich out of that trip.

"At another time, I had an engagement more than ten miles from where my forenoon preaching was to take place. The services at this place were appointed for half-past six in the evening. The roads were fearful and I had no conveyance except my feet. At about half-past three, I started for my appointment. At seven o'clock with my face showing that I had not had an easy time of it, I appeared before the anxiously waiting crowd and imparted my message. They appreciated my labors highly and were anxious for me to preach for them often, and so they thought that they would give me a lift. They made a raise of one dollar and sixty cents, and they thought they might do more next time. (Such is the wonderfully exciting life of a College Beggar.)"

Fund Raising Is Living in Suspense

"During the two years begging labors, on the whole I have found a generous and hospitable reception. But among so many, it must not be thought strange if we are made to see some of the less favorable sides of humanity. And not a few expedients must be invented to get money from those who are not inclined. One following this work is living in suspense most all the time. He does not know how many snobs, grouts, and hogs he will have to encounter during the week ahead. He cannot know how long he will have to wait before Mr. Slowberry gets ready to give an answer. He does not know how many will take him for an imposter, and show not a few signs of suspicion. The rock beds of penuriousness and greed of money-lenders are not familiar to him until he has been over the world in some such capacity.

"When one has seen enough of the human race to distinguish between its peculiar traits, he can tell to whom he can devote time and whom it is best to drop. There are most always some in a town who should be put on the 'drop list.' The excuses so freely uttered, and the 'ifs' so often spoken have become fixed in my memory, and those who have put forth their 'ifs' are by no means forgotten.

"Without having the trouble that we sometimes give them, we have learned how many people are measured—what their neighbors think of them. We have found that, while human nature, as to its essence, is the same throughout the world, there are many peculiarities widely differing. We have seen those who are pious, and those who are worldly; those who have cant in abundance, and those who have the genuine article we have also seen.

"Considering the fact that mankind has been obliged to climb up from the lowest stages of savagery and imperfections, we ought to congratulate ourselves that there is so much promise for a still higher human development and to that end we should use the means placed in our hands to further the intellectual and spiritual culture of all who need the light and force so useful to mankind."

Chapter Fifteen

A Call to Service

In the depth and quiet of our souls, do we confront ourselves by asking questions about our roles as fund raising volunteers or professionals? Do we ask why we are here?

"Is it a trip, just a job, or something to satisfy our ego because we are playing with someone else's money or associating with the community's elite?" a testy volunteer challenged me during a school campaign years ago. "What's in it for you? What do you want to get out of all of this? Tell me, is this just a lark for you? Or is it a selfish opportunity to get close to big money and to hobnob with the city's elite?"

Service Is Investment of Self

Service can be defined as the selfless process of investing ourselves, our energies, our talents, and our spirit to serve the public good. Others have put it into more poetic language. Wordsworth, in a sonnet entitled "Afterthought," reminds us, "Enough, if something from our hands have power/To live, and act, and serve the future hour." Or consider Cicero's dictum that "by sharing the joy of another we increase it, by sharing the woe of another we diminish it." And Emily Dickinson wrote, "If I can stop one Heart from breaking/I shall not live in vain/If I can ease one Life the Aching/Or cool one Pain/Or help one fainting Robin/Unto his nest again/I shall not live in Vain."

What is in it for us? A deeply felt satisfaction at accomplishment of a task in support of a mission that will touch many people in the future or the thrill of meeting the goal when the consensus argued that it was impossible.

Our service is to look at a problem, to survey it critically, to do research to determine whether or not the job can be done. If it can be done, we prepare a plan. We develop strategies; we assert ourselves to encourage financial support. We brief the executive. We train staff and volunteers in the solicitation process. We solicit gifts when it is necessary. We negotiate with financial officers. We celebrate successes; we bemoan failures. We applaud or we chastise staff or volunteers. We encourage donors to give and, possibly, to increase their gifts. And, yes, in weaker moments, we are prone to boast quietly to our egos, "Hey, look at me and see what I can do." We are human after all.

It might be said that all of this is just a job for skilled professionals, and I would agree that the bare-bones job is that. But there is much to be done beyond the basic job, and it is the servant leaders (Greenleaf, 1991) who go beyond basic requirements, beyond what is expected, beyond what may be seen as necessary to ensure the attainment of the final goal. Theirs is service beyond the pale.

As fund raisers, we are sensitive professionals, not just technical practitioners. We are reflective in our service, and we are servant leaders to the community, to the donors, to the clients who need the services of our organizations. The word servant in this context is not demeaning; it does not diminish our professional image. It does require us to ask ourselves at regular intervals those penetrating questions: Am I doing my job right? Am I fulfilling my responsibility to the institution?

Illustrations

A young development officer with a theology school visited an aged widow once a week for two years. It was necessary for him to drive seventy miles in each direction. When he arrived at his destination, he performed many tasks for the elderly widow that were difficult for her to perform. He took splendid care of the woman for several years. After her death, the seminary was notified that she had bequeathed $1 million dollars to the school's endowment. Cynics said that the development officer knew that would happen and that is why he drove the distance every week. My feeling is that this young person was a true servant leader, someone who understood the needs of a lonely soul and was willing to devote himself to her service. He had no assurance that the bequest would be made.

An older fund raising consultant was sitting at home, relaxing one evening when the telephone rang. The caller, a person that the consultant did not know, said, "Will you please come to my home? I want to make a gift to your organization. Can you come tonight?"

It was a difficult request to set aside, yet the consultant had a vague image of the neighborhood to which he was being summoned, and he suspected that the gift would be small—perhaps $50 or $100. When he reached and surveyed the neighborhood, the top figure dropped to $50, and when he arrived at the home of the caller and saw a sign on the front lawn with the words "Child Care Services," his sights dropped to about $15 or $25. He smiled and said to himself, "Well, it has been a pleasant ride and perhaps the conversation will be interesting."

Several hours later, after a pleasant visit, the host brought up the primary subject. He explained that the thought of a gift had been on his mind for some months, and he handed the consultant a check for $125,000. After the consultant regained his composure, he explained that he would send the donor an official receipt that he could use to claim a tax deduction. The donor said, "You can do that, but no rush. I have exceeded my tax deductions for the year."

There are many surprises in this business of fund raising—a good number of them pleasant ones, designed, I suppose, to sustain our resolve to stay with the profession.

Many volunteers are equally committed to serving their organizations. Here are just three of the many examples I could report.

During a door-to-door solicitation for a capital campaign in California, one of the volunteers was the wife of a popular congressman. On a rainy day, I encountered her out on a street, wet and cold. "For heaven's sake, what are you doing?" I asked. "I did not expect you to canvass today. It's too wet."

"That's my strategy," she said. "People feel sorry for me and immediately invite me into their home. We have a pleasant conversation, and," she grinned, "I get a generous gift in every home!"

For another capital campaign, this one for the Rescue Mission, Syracuse, New York, in 1953, the campaign chair was a prominent business leader in Syracuse, a brusque and direct person. As soon as he accepted the assignment, he gave $25,000. Then he said, "Let's go talk to a friend of mine. I'll ask him to match me." His friend was one of the owners of a flourishing department store, and his retort to our chair's request for $25,000 was quick and blunt. "You must be out of your mind. You want me to give $25,000 to those bums who wallow in wine and sleep in the gutter? You want that I should give money to help them?" The last statement was a shout. Our chair quietly answered, "The difference between them and us is we pay more for our wine. Cool down, buddy. It's only $25,000, only worth five bottles of your wine." The gift was received several weeks later. It was for $15,000.

For a capital campaign I have mentioned before, to raise money to build a hospital in the Santa Clara Valley, we planned a house-to-house canvass, with the expectation that we would not raise much money by this method. The goal for the entire valley of six communities was simply $25,000. A woman, a member of the board, volunteered to solicit. She inquired about the goal. She said, "That's fair." Two weeks later, she reported in with $25,000 in gifts. She had misunderstood. The goal for her community was only $8,000. Obviously, we ended up oversubscribing the county goal.

Are we bound fully and intellectually to the job? Are we committed to that phenomenon that Robert Payton (1988) refers to as the "social history of the moral imagination, *philanthropy*" (p. 71)?

Payton teases us with the question—"Do you live *for* or do you live *off* of philanthropy?" The critical question has to be, Are we truly dedicated in service to the organization that has hired or retained us and to the donors who want to serve the organization with their gifts? If we are, our primary duty is to serve the donors responsibly. By doing so, we are serving the organization well.

We should heed Robert Coles's account of six-year-old Tessie. Tessie was one of four African American girls who initiated school desegregation in New Orleans in 1961, fighting her way through angry, threatening mobs every day for months, escorted through a gauntlet of terror by federal marshals. Much later, she rationalized the terror-filled experience to Coles this way: "Those people have gone back home, and they don't mind their kids coming to school with us anymore. So that's what we were supposed to do. We were supposed to get them to stop being so angry, then they would quiet down and we would have desegregation. So we did the service we

were supposed to do in New Orleans. Next, it'll be some other thing
to do, because, you always should be trying to help out God somehow" (Coles, 1993, p. 7).

Are We Responding to a Call?

Consider these six questions: Who are we? Why do we exist? What
is distinctive about us? What do we intend to accomplish? How do
we plan to do it? How will we hold ourselves accountable? Can we
answer these questions with Tessie's admonition, which she said
she learned from her grandmother, "You always should be trying
to help out God somehow"? Should we respond further that fund
raising is the servant of philanthropy and, therefore, a servant to
the community? By association, then, are we not servants to philanthropic fund raising?

In performing our service are we responding to a calling? Or does
that idea give us moral pause? Having a calling is part of our legacy,
part of the fragile fabric that has been entrusted to our care. When
we serve this legacy, we do become both servants and leaders. I have
just talked about what we are as servants. What are we as leaders?

Fund Raising as a Profession

As leaders, we ought to be learned professionals, accepted as such
by our society. It may be that we should walk the same path as es-
teemed members of the classic professions: doctors, lawyers, clergy-
men, engineers, accountants, and others. What would it mean to us
to do this? What is professionalism? How does one identify a professional? And how do we ourselves walk and talk like professionals?

Out of the writings of Bloland and Bornstein (1991), Carbone
(1989), Houle (1960), Etzioni (1969), and others, certain criteria
emerge. However, Bloland and Bornstein (p. 120) observe that
"although there is considerable interest in professional status in
the fund raising occupation, it is primarily the association of professionalization with legitimacy that interests fund raisers. Even as
they see themselves as professionals, fund raisers do not see development as a mature profession."

There are some good reasons for these feelings among fund
raisers. For example, consider the locus of authority within the non-

profit organization. The authority to initiate a fund raising program resides in the board of trustees. Because the raising of money affects the assets of the nonprofit and its budget, the board of trustees holds the final authority for any action that in any way will affect the assets or the budget. The line of command that the development officer must follow is first to the chief executive and from that executive to the board. The professional fund raising staff has no authority other than what has been passed down to them from the board. This is downward communication and many complications are inherent in it, bringing more complexity to what is already a difficult task. In addition, the board is too often hesitant to accept any responsibility for the fund raising program and, therefore, is not in a strong position to lend its wisdom to the execution of the planned strategies. Board communications often are couched in negative tones that tend to depress the mood of staff members.

The locus of authority in nonprofits may also be one of the reasons for what is called the eighteen-month syndrome, that is, short-term employment, on the part of younger practitioners. Having less control than desired over decisions, receiving low financial incentives, and lacking sanctioning power over staff members or volunteers who violate established norms of behavior may also contribute to low commitment to norms of service and fewer members than desirable remaining in the fund raising profession throughout their lifetimes.

Fund raisers do not spend too much time considering whether professional status has a positive impact on the ability of the development staff to meet financial goals or to control their work patterns. Development staff members' abilities, their understanding of the scope and complexities of the work, and their relationships with the executive staff, the development committee, and board members may seem the greatest determinant of the amount of jurisdiction they have over their work. Nor do they often see a connection between bottom-line effectiveness in fund raising and the generation of theory and research. The essence of professionalism in fund raising has been possessing an appropriate knowledge base, being able to apply that knowledge to the work, and being able to interact and to work pleasantly with other people.

However, this is beginning to change. The transfer of The Fund Raising School to Indiana University in 1988 actuated the establishment of that institution's Center on Philanthropy, under the direction of Robert Payton. Payton moved quickly to encourage basic research, with the intent to expand the theoretical base available to support courses in the study of philanthropy and fund raising. It seems it now is up to fund raising practitioners to decide how far and in which direction the pursuit of professionalization will go. There is strong support for on-the-job and association-sponsored training programs to promote the professional progress of fund raisers. Bloland and Bornstein express the concern that the existing knowledge base—developing though it may be—comprises mechanical knowledge, that is, technical tools to explain the how-to's of fund raising—and precious little of the theoretical base that would help us to respond to questions that ask why. A body of technical knowledge, no matter how complete, how well authenticated, or how aged, will never lift us to the learned ranks of the classic professions.

But the Indiana University Center on Philanthropy and other university-based centers are moving to broaden academic research in philanthropy and fund raising. This activity is expanding the theoretical knowledge base supporting an increasing number of academic studies in the field at Indiana University and at the University of San Francisco, Case Western University, and many other schools. A recent roster of centers of philanthropy and centers of study and research in philanthropy lists more than forty throughout the United States, Mexico, Australia, Sweden, Canada, and England. More are on the way.

If we are to move assertively to higher levels, becoming members of a recognized, universally accepted, *learned* profession, we must acknowledge the need for a unified effort, a unity of the spirits of those who profess to be professional. Today, we are not united; we are splintered. We have an assemblage of specialties, organizational and trade. We have as associations the American Association of Fund-Raising Counsel (AAFRC), the Association of Healthcare Philanthropy (AHCP), the Association of Lutheran Development Executives (ALDE), Advanced Certified Fund Raising Executives (ACFRE), the Association for Prospect Research (APR), the Council for the Advancement and Support of Education (CASE), the Certified Fund Raising Executives (CFRE), the National Association of YMCA Development Officers (NAYDO), the National Committee on Planned Giving (NCPG), the National Society of Fund Raising Executives (NSFRE), and perhaps others that I do not know about. Most of these associations have their own membership enlistment processes and their own codes of ethics. Thus, instead of a growing like a single strong tree, we are isolated splinters of what could be a giant majestic redwood or a solid oak. Our national voice is weakened by different interpretations and by the lack of a coordinated front.

There is no denying the need for some separate identities. There are individual and organizational fund raising specialties. A merger of these individual missions may not be appropriate. We can work, however, toward a more united front on such issues as achieving greater professional status, reaching higher levels of professional acknowledgment, striving for greater acceptance and authentication by academia, and earning respect from governmental and regulatory bodies that have a confused sense of who, what, and why we are. Our segmented voices do not add to the strength of our profession's national voice in the halls of Congress, in regulatory offices, or in the public arena.

Doctors, lawyers, accountants, nurses, and others have both a national body (the American Medical Association and the American Bar Association, for example) and bodies representing individual specialties. The overarching society in each case draws strength from the mass of its own members, it does not attempt a roll call of the special groups. Carbone (1989, p. 46) maintains that fund raising is an occupation that has moved steadily along the professional continuum, *an occupation with the potential to attain greater professional stature.* "In all candor," he writes, "true professional status for fund raisers may be an unreachable star, but greater professional stature is certainly possible. . . . Fund raisers can accelerate progress along the professional continuum and thus hasten fund raising's professional maturity." Perhaps middle-status groups such as schoolteachers, nurses, social workers, librarians, *and fund raisers,* should work to improve their status to middle-professional ranks rather than strive for full professional recognition. Or perhaps it is even irrelevant whether or not we ever become a part of the classic professions or whether or not fund raising is ever accepted as a learned profession or a semi-profession. *What is important is how we see ourselves.* We ought to see ourselves as professionals, in our ethical structure, the values we believe in and espouse, our acceptance of the privilege of the public trust, and our selfless commitment to the mission that we serve.

Robert Bellah quarrels with the observation of Thomas Haskell in *The Emergence of the Professional Social Scientist* that "the new man of science has to exchange general citizenship in society for membership in the community of the competent." Bellah retorts:

> The competent social scientist does not have to cease to be a "general citizen of society." Specialization requires integration; they are not mutually exclusive. A professional social science that loses concern for the larger society cannot do even its professional job, for there is too much of reality with which it cannot deal. And if we remember that "calling" or "vocation," with the implications of public responsibility, is the older meaning of the word "profession," then we would see that a really "professional social scientist," could never be only a specialist. He would also see social science as, in part, public philosophy [1985, pp. 299–300].

And so it is, I say, with philanthropy and its obedient servant, the profession, the vocation, the calling of philanthropic fund raising. Philanthropy is in part public philosophy.

For many years, I have cherished a dream that together we could gird our profession with a steel and rock integrity so that it could be a bulwark to our efforts to practice and to teach philanthropy throughout the land.

What is required?

The first requirement is an expanded base of theoretical knowledge, resulting from academically qualified research, and use of that knowledge to support a core curriculum for undergraduate and graduate studies. That is the reason I founded The Fund Raising School in 1974, to instigate training at the basic level as a spur to more and more advanced studies at higher levels.

Another requirement is the availability of academic credit studies in philanthropy and philanthropic fund raising for practicing professionals, for trustees, and for nonprofit administrators. This campus-based knowledge and development experience could support programs of study meeting in high schools, in churches, in business establishments, and in service organizations.

A further requirement is advanced studies for the more senior professional. Since many of these professionals cannot easily leave their bases, these studies could be electronically facilitated through computer disks and videocassettes and enhanced by regularly scheduled on-campus seminars and symposia. Courses would be taught by a combination of qualified academic faculty and reflective peers.

Professional certification or accreditation is a requirement and would be designed by an overarching professional commission. The certification examination would test each applicant's understanding of the extensive body of professional knowledge. The examination would require written responses to questions that would challenge the aspirants' ability to think conceptually about the role of philanthropy both in the national and in the world society. It would cause the aspiring candidates to study such subjects as the psychology of associations, human behavior, political strategies, strategic planning, nonprofit management, and so forth. Questions would also examine the relationship of fund raising and philanthropy, fund raising and the community, fund raising and our global society, and fund raising and the law. Ethical issues relating to fund raising are a matter of great concern to the marketplace as well as among practicing professionals. Candidates' understanding of the ethical structure of fund raising would be addressed, possibly through the use of case studies. This subject must continue to hold a top-of-the-agenda position in the profession. In short, the certification examination would rigorously test the candidates' broad knowledge of the techniques, the philosophy, and the ethical base undergirding philanthropy and its hard-working servant, fund raising.

The certification commission would be pan-professional, comprising selected senior practitioners from each of the major societies. Territorial concerns would be set aside, thus acknowledging the need for a unified certification process. Academic cooperation could be sought to develop and to administer the certification test.

This certification process will provide a certain level of gatekeeping for the profession. It will project fund raising's professional heritage and its coming of age as a mature, responsible, accountable profession. A unified code of ethics with thoughtfully defined sanctions will attest to our capacity as trustworthy practitioners to police ourselves. We will strive to become reflective practitioners.

Fund raising can be a profession, a vocation, a ministry, or a calling—or it can be just a job. It must, it can, and it should require the best from each of us. Accreditation will test our aptitude as scholars of philanthropy, and it will test our resolve, our commitment to service, and our integrity.

Can we do a responsible job of regulating ourselves? As mentioned in Chapter Five, Congressman Jake Pickel, in a September 1993 report to the oversight subcommittee of the House Ways and Means Committee, stated that of the more than one million 990AR financial reports filed annually by 501(c)(3) organizations with the Internal Revenue Service, only 1 to 2 percent are read by IRS staff. How many of these reports are read by state authorities, we have to wonder, when cross-filed with states with regulatory statutes? Do we need more of this costly emptiness?

The federal government continues to discuss the matter of licensing professional fund raising people. Will licensing cause us to be more trustworthy, more responsible, more accountable? It seems to me the ethical structure of this profession, our long heritage of philanthropy, the volume of service given unselfishly by volunteers every day, and the overwhelming generosity of our donors should compel us to function as ethical beings. We should be eager and honored to give service to the best of our ability to a cause that touches so many people around the world. It is a privilege to be able to serve.

Conclusion

The future is coming up before us. Heed the words about the future from the Iroquois: "Look behind you. See your sons and your daughters. They are your future. Look further, and see your sons' and your daughters' children and their children's children even unto the Seventh Generation. That's the way we were taught. Think about it: you, yourself are a Seventh Generation!" (Arden and Wall, 1990, p. 120).

We have a rich heritage that has been passed to us over the millennia to cherish and then to pass on. As fund raisers, nonprofit executives, donors, trustees, volunteers, and philanthropists, we must consider the Seventh Generation. The fragile fabric of philanthropy must be passed on intact to the generations ahead. I have already spoken about our need for gatekeepers for our profession. We should give equal, or perhaps greater, attention to keeping our gateways open to those who are qualified to join our profession and who want to become enthusiastic partners in our work.

We must turn our attention to attracting young children and high school students, informing them about the philosophy and significance of philanthropy and the basic principles of giving and raising money for proper causes. We can invite them to National Philanthropy Day observances. Give them philanthropic projects to carry out. Offer prizes for the best posters, poems, and essays about philanthropy, with the provision that part of the prize will be given to a nonprofit of their choice. We could select the young philanthropist or fund raiser of the year.

Moreover, we must let people know that the welcome sign is out for women, ethnic minorities, and young and old, to join our work to advance the cause of philanthropy.

Let us keep the gateways to philanthropy open to all and be ready to receive them when they come.

References

American Association of Fund-Raising Counsel. *Giving USA 1995.* New York: AAFRC Trust for Philanthropy, 1995.

Arden, H., and Wall, S. *Wisdomkeepers.* Hillsboro, Oreg.: Beyond Words, 1990.

Bellah, R. N., and others. *Habits of the Heart.* Berkeley: University of California Press, 1985.

Bloland, H., and Bornstein, R. "Fund Raising in Transition." In D. Burlingame and L. J. Hulse (eds.), *Taking Fund Raising Seriously: Advancing the Profession and Practice of Raising Money.* San Francisco: Jossey-Bass, 1991.

Bremner, R. H. *American Philanthropy.* (2nd ed.) Chicago: University of Chicago Press, 1988.

Bryson, J. M. *Strategic Planning for Public and Nonprofit Organizations: A Guide to Strengthening and Sustaining Organizational Achievement.* San Francisco: Jossey-Bass, 1988.

Carbone, R. *"Fund Raising as a Profession,"* College Park, Md.: Clearinghouse for Research on Fund Raising, 1989.

Charles, C. *Leadership.* San Francisco: Fund Raising School, 1974.

Coles, R. *The Call of Service: A Witness to Idealism.* Boston: Houghton Mifflin, 1993.

Conway, D. *The Good Steward,* Louisville, Ky.: Conway, 1994.

Cutlip, S. M. *Fund Raising in the United States: Its Role in America's Philanthropy.* New Brunswick, N.J.: Rutgers University Press, 1965.

Drucker, P. F. "Post-Capitalist Society." Harvard Business Review, Sept.–Oct. 1992.

Etzioni, A. *The Semi-Professions and Their Organizations: Teachers, Nurses, and Social Workers.* New York: Free Press, 1969.

Greenleaf, R. K. *The Servant as Leader.* Indianapolis: Robert K. Greenleaf Center for Servant-Leadership, 1991.

Hesselbein, F., Goldsmith, M., and Beckhard, R. (eds.). *The Leader of the Future.* San Francisco: Jossey-Bass, 1996.

Houle, C. O. *The Effective Board.* New York: Association Press, 1960.

Joseph, J. A. *Remaking America: How the Benevolent Traditions of Many Cultures Are Transforming Our National Life.* San Francisco: Jossey-Bass, 1995.

LeBoeuf, M. *How to Win Customers and Keep Them for Life.* New York: Berkley, 1987.

Mather, C. *Essays to Do Good.* Boston: Green, 1710.

Mullin, R. *The Wealth of Christians.* Maryknoll, N.Y.: Orbis Books, 1984.

Payton, R. L. *Philanthropy: Voluntary Action for the Public Good.* Old Tappan, N.J.: Macmillan, 1988.

Seymour, H. J. *Designs for Fund-Raising.* New York: McGraw-Hill, 1966.

Smith, C. *Corporate Philanthropy Report.* Alexandria, Va.: Capitol, 1994.

Smith, J. H. "Honorable Beggars: The Middlemen of American Philanthropy." Unpublished thesis, University of Wisconsin, 1968.

Index